WHAT TO FEEL, HOW TO FEEL

Palimpsest Press
1171 Eastlawn Ave.
Windsor, Ontario. N8S 3J1
www.palimpsestpress.ca

Printed and bound in Canada
Cover design and book typography by Ellie Hastings
Edited by Jim Johnstone

Palimpsest Press would like to thank the Canada Council for the Arts and the Ontario Arts Council for their support of our publishing program. We also acknowledge the assistance of the Government of Ontario through the Ontario Book Publishing Tax Credit.

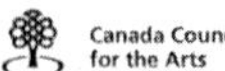

Canada

LIBRARY AND ARCHIVES CANADA CATALOGUING IN PUBLICATION

TITLE: What to feel, how to feel: lyric essays on neurodivergence and neurofatherhood / Shane Neilson.
NAMES: Neilson, Shane, 1975- author
IDENTIFIERS: Canadiana (print) 20250179474
Canadiana (ebook) 20250182866

ISBN 9781990293948 (SOFTCOVER)
ISBN 9781990293986 (EPUB)
SUBJECTS: LCSH: Neilson, Shane, 1975-—Mental health. | LCSH: Neurodiversity—Social aspects. | LCSH: Neurodivergent people—Family relationships. | LCSH: Discrimination in medical care. | LCSH: Autistic people—Social conditions. | LCSH: Fathers and sons. | LCSH: Fatherhood. | LCGFT: Essays.

CLASSIFICATION: LCC HV1570.23 .N45 2025 | DDC 616.85/882—DC2

WHAT TO FEEL, HOW TO FEEL:

LYRIC ESSAYS ON NEURODIVERGENCE AND NEUROFATHERHOOD

SHANE NEILSON

TABLE OF CONTENTS

For Lynn, Janet Ann, Corey, and Dr. J

We normals develop conceptions, whether objectively grounded or not, as to the sphere of life-activity for which an individual's particular stigma primarily disqualifies him

— Erving Goffman

the huge
tire of a truck, split open,
glowed, its body blacker than the black
shadows, and blackest was the dark inside
its wound

— Al Moritz, "Given"

DIFFERENTIAL

Maybe someone like me comes along, and you feel it before you see it, or you see it and then suddenly feel it; you see it and feel, *Hey, he's different.* Like obscenity, you know when difference is in your presence. You said *retard*, you said *quad*, you said *weirdo*, you said it again and again and again.

I'll come wearing loose-fitting clothes somehow ill-suited to my body, my face on one of two settings (blankness or anger), and my voice will, despite a formal articulateness, seem livid. I'll speak at length, endlessly riffing on the variations of an idea and its effects. I'll wear you out. I'll wear you down. I'm not able to tell. You'll leave or object; then I will feel the usual shame, the familiar chronic misunderstanding. Why couldn't things be different?

The sadness is—they cannot be. The world is not that way.

The sadness is—I am different.

The world is at a variance to me, but I see it, I feel it. Therein is the difficulty, an aspirational one. If I can see and sense the world, then why can it not welcome me?

The strangest quality about being different—a difference signalled early on by others but only tragically understood later—is unfoldingness, constant becoming and unbecoming. Only by ignoring what I call the "differential constant," meaning how I affect others and how others affect me, could mutually constructed difference become simple. Stigma makes things easy for you. Stigma means I am bad and you are good.

Difference is the condition I've known my entire life. Once upon a time, I was on a panel struck by the Physician's Health Program of Ontario. Each of the gathered physician panellists retailed their personal histories as if they were a testimonial to the merits of overcoming struggle, their episodic challenges mere way stations to a better life, detours that somehow invested the future with greater brightness. Their accounts proceeded like this:

> *At some point in my medical training, I got sick due to either mental illness or addiction.*
>
> > *I couldn't work.*
> >
> > *It was very bad.*
> >
> > *I felt very bad.*
> >
> > *But I enrolled in the Physician's Health Program, and got better.*
> >
> > *Now I can work!*
> >
> > *And the work I do is informed by the struggle I went through.*

I am a better physician for the experience!

After hearing this repetitive misvoicing of disability, a telling of disability warped through the medical model, I said: "Rather than give a history in which I entered medical training, got ill, then got better again so that I could return to successful practise, I've been living out as a weirdo for years!" And the truth is, I've always been strange. To honour all the neurodivergent people out there—here's to the four points, the corners we've stood in, our innings in not-normal—let me tell this story instead:

I've always been what you'd call unwell or different.

My experience has never been one of normality.

I'm the son of a mentally ill alcoholic.

I've experienced illness periodically my entire life.

I took pleasure in confessing to biomedicine's clerics that I was non-normative long before entering medical school, that I was unwell in medical school itself, and during my residency, quite ill. Though I too enrolled in the Physician's Health Program eventually, and returned to practice like my other panellists, I did so without eradicating the substance of my disability, its character or mark.

I've always been unwell to a biomedical way of thinking, and that's why, in this book, I'm going to speak about ableism, the stultifying force that polices my difference. Though it takes many forms, and can be well-intentioned, it is the reason that freedom, the quality I've sought all my life, is impossible. The world normalizes, we normalize, we prefer the things that are like. We prefer what we like, versions of us, reflections staring back. Reciprocity. Predictability. When we say we all share the fact of humanity, we say, as individuals: I love myself and I want to be happy with all the other mes, let there be a cavalcade of mes, all of us rightly desperate to be with me.

Jerome Mazzaro points out that the title of Robert Lowell's *Land of Unlikeness,* his first book from 1944, is ripped from a quotation of Saint Bernard; he further explains that the quote pertains to the "human's soul's unlikeness to God and unlikeness to its past self."

The human soul, often exclusionary and mean, finds distraction in baubles and screens. We all seek the same thing—beauty. The clouds move by my window hour after hour, each one made of the same material, and yet unlike the last. I have never seen a human soul, but I have detected the darkness in bodies. Perhaps seeing a soul, seeing the "human," is a condition of normativity?

Difference is more than wistfulness. Difference is never accepting the abuse that comes while being powerless to stop it. No one can right the misalignment in the universe because the misalignment is actually a correction. Call us anomalies, disruptions, glitches—we're the dark matter you need to make your universe make sense. We're paradisical rupture. We who cannot speak like you, to you, are perceived as constituted of lack. But you lack comprehension, for difference is not lack. You need us to be perfect? First of all, you are not perfect. Second: your brand of perfection is an oppressive prison, and you need us to inform you of your lack of freedom. You need us to free you though we can never be free from you.

God, I often hate all the likes, all the little likes running around liking their preferred likes, their stock of likes, operating within a stockade excluding the unlikes.

In "Not in Kansas" by The National, a female chorus sings:

Time has come now to stop being human
Time to find a new creature to be
Be a fish or a weed or a sparrow
For the earth has grown tired and all of your time has expired

We're not exactly new. But being more like us could be a new experience for you.

In the fall of 2019, I've been—finally, after avoiding the prospect for decades—diagnosed as being on the autism spectrum. Though the diagnosis makes much-consolidating sense of my life—the "key" metaphor is accurate—it also means I must manage the confused feelings brought about by being, to a particular manner of thinking, precisely what the stigmatizing figures I've encountered in my life said I was.

Stupid.

Retard.

Moron.

Idiot.

Rain Man.

Rain Man.

Rain Man.

I mutter this exact phrase under my breath when no one is looking: I-am-a-stupid-retard-moron-idiot-Rain-Man.

In high school, Rain Man was my nickname. I never told anyone after I escaped that place.

Charlie (Tom Cruise) in *Rain Man*: Raymond, what are you looking at? The ducks are over here. What are you looking at?

Raymond (Dustin Hoffman): I don't know.

When a publisher commissioned this book over a lunch, he said, "We're looking to publish diverse works, and you are definitely the right kind of guy to write a book about ableism, what it's like to walk around every day as someone different." When I submitted the book, he said, "It's too angry. I can't publish it." An hour later, he introduced me to an audience at a reading and said, "The first time I met him, I was kind of afraid of him."

Stigma pre-sets its traps. Once stigma is instilled—in other words, once someone who is non-able-body-minded is indoctrinated in normativity—one's always working against pain. We feel the label. Our difference is now negative identity, a corruption of being. We deserve abuse according to such logic. We, more than anyone else, know how much we are not like the likes.

Pre-set trap: any job interview I have ever participated in.

Since I am stigmatized, the trap is that I feel I need to fight back. To the cunning stigmatizers out there, a target's resistance to stigmatization confirms the need for further discrimination. Writing out the workings of this mechanism, even though I'm only doing so in summary, calls forth a pain so deep and lasting that it is hard, when writing this sentence, to do so without being overcome, thereby calling into being the trap itself, the impulse to offload negative affect by "doing something." So much harder to become and unbecome; so much easier to try to destigmatize the world, to challenge and fight, to detonate.

Pre-set trap: meeting any girlfriend's parents.

I first heard the word "different" in New Brunswick, but rather than focus on the stigmatizing instances when it was used as an epithet, I want to tell you about the moment I heard, for the first time, the word uttered to signify a protected space where such difference was appreciated, tolerated, and even respected.

When I was twenty-six years old, locked up in a hospital, a kind psychiatrist named Devarajan asked my brother, "What was he like as a child?" Corey is younger, bigger, stronger, and faster than me; the only advantage I have over him is intelligence, and even then, we're talking a splinter intelligence, a narrow range of capabilities that cohere around language. Corey eventually said, "Well, he's always been different."

Devarajan followed up. "What do you mean? What kind of different?"

Corey didn't have the vocabulary to explain *exactly* what he meant. At that time, neither did I. But let me recall for you what the intonation meant to me. Corey spoke matter-of-factly, without rancour, as if the issue of difference had long been the case, but also something that would continue to be. Without embarrassment, seemingly without shame, he spoke then the way I would like to speak about stigma now. If I am ever able to speak like him, embracing difference (done) but also letting go of the damage caused by stigma (not done, and perhaps never), then I think I will have become and un-become at a final moulting.

Pre-set trap: entering an unfamiliar space.

I find it impossible to render difference without being in conversation with pain, but it is my hope that this inability will prove to be part of a further becoming and un-becoming.

Pre-set trap: ordering food in a restaurant.

Talking to a doctor.

Talking to my children's teachers.

Setting foot outside my house.

I offer a lyric description of a life spent on the wrong end of stigma—my life. I write to change attitudes, to create the conditions for a great kindness, one that might assist or comfort the ill and disabled. I write for the little boy I was, undefended against a stigmatizing system that predicated the entirety of its operations on shame. That little boy had no idea how pitiless the world could be, and so I write to change the world for that same little boy and for the millions of children who continue to suffer in their difference.

I write, paradoxically, of *sameness*, of shared vulnerability, and I write in much the same tone as one of my favourite poets, Milton Acorn, who was ill somewhat like I am ill.

Acorn once wrote, "for love and pain, love and pain / are companions in this age." I titled my PhD dissertation on chronic pain in Canadian literature, *Companions in This Age.*

Love and pain are both like and unlike; do you see? It is where we can meet, difference and norm.

I write in love and anger. I write to you, the average ableist, the *Normie*; and to you, the neurodivergent.

Trap sprung:

SECTION ONE:

CHASING GOFFMAN

ON STIGMA

Run.

*

Rub my father's burnt particulates between thumb and forefinger, or let go? With the bluest sky staring down onto a grass-green bridge overhanging the wide Wolastoq, I resolved to live the rest of my life extending compassion to those oppressed by stigma. Then the ashes were taken by the wind—I do not know if they landed where my father wanted, the river he claimed to love. All my life, I could never be sure he loved a single thing, even himself. Perhaps he was never permitted to love himself. Thinking that, I made myself a promise. Since there would be no ridding myself of him, I needed to renovate the places where he still inhabited me.

*

The Greeks, who were apparently strong on visual aids, originated the term stigma to refer to bodily signs designed to expose something unusual and bad about the moral status of the signifier.

*

Oh, invisible defect, as an invisible defective, I sing this song for you.

*

A book published by my aunt, *Sheffield Memories*, is the only history of the Neilson clan.

Beneath its royal blue cover, this book contains genealogical information as well as local community facts, but for me, there are two essential pages. On one, a black-and-white picture of my eight-year-old father, Douglas Neilson, stares out. So small, his hand holding the chain suspension of a swing set, standing at the end beside his sisters, glare forcing him to squint. I know exactly where the picture was taken based on backdrop: my grandfather's farm, in front of Ralph's large barn, but a version that seems impossibly new. Flipping to the second essential page, there's an aerial photo of the Neilson farm along the banks of the Saint John, taken in winter 1958, a short time before my father joined the army:

Neilson farm, 1958

This is the inception point, the earliest documentary evidence of Doug as he was, unmediated by tainted tale. Other than these two images, one of which isn't even of him but of his place, I possess only fourth-hand accounts from others, for my father would not speak to me of his childhood. I have stared for the equivalent of days at this picture, trying to divine if Doug's difference was manifest in posture or gaze, by facial expression or just simple energy. Of course *I* can see it—but only because we are the same. I either project myself into him or overvalue what I interpret as his sensory recoil from the sun, the hopeful yet baffled affect the picture exudes, as if he is making something and being told *No*, that he should *Never*.

*

Instruction in shame begins at birth. Families subscribing to the "system" believe that the overriding explanation for all unwanted behaviour in children comes from badness. The adjective for the non-normative child may not be "bad" in these families, the rhetorical program for control more euphemistic; different families have varying levels of sophistication for their system. Yet the consistent method is to blame the child for any perceived or invented transgression so that the child can feel bad, thereby encouraging them to agree with their abuser that they are indeed wrong and deserve punishment. The child becomes the abuser's creature when their identity internalizes shame. Furthermore, because the child cannot anticipate the desires of those in power, the child must agree that, in addition, they are stupid. Survival necessitates internalization. There is stupidity and there is badness. In terms of chronology, since the bad child was bad before, the child is bad in the present too, and will only be so in the future. Because their worthlessness is both pre-existing and future-oriented, shame is inescapable. No matter where you look, no matter when, shame parents that child.

*

That which can be always told about an individual's social identity during his daily round and by all persons he encounters therein will be of great importance to him. The consequence of a presentation that is performance made to the public at large may be small in particular contacts, but in every contact there will be some consequences, which, taken together, can be immense... [t]hus, any change in the way the individual must always and everywhere present himself will for these very reasons be fateful—this presumably providing the Greeks with the idea of stigma in the first place.

*

New Brunswick in the early 1980s was not supportive of sufferers. I remember overhearing casual jokes about Centracare, the provincial "nut house" located in Lancaster. Such rhetoric teaches children that to be ill is to be bad. But what could it have been like for my father, growing up in rural New Brunswick in the 1940s and 1950s? Worse. A distinguishing fact about Doug: as a child his parents took him to a psychiatrist due to his abnormal behaviour. Based on my research, there was exactly *one* of these practising in Fredericton at the time, helming a mental health clinic created as part of the then-burgeoning de-institutionalization movement. A particular focus of the clinic was testing the mental capacity of children and establishing whether they were "mentally defective" or not.

*

My half-sister bears secret knowledge. Recently, she told me of mythical possible letters my father wrote home from Baden, Germany, when he was in the Canadian Forces. He was sixteen years old, enlisting despite being a minor because he could not be managed by his family. She remembers being told by someone when she was just a child herself—she cannot remember who—that our father wrote letter after letter from overseas to Sadie, his mother, about men shoving him into a barrel and rolling him down hills, sometimes whacking the barrel with sticks. My sister and I both want those letters so that we can learn what he was like in his own words, perhaps get a glimpse of him before stigma claimed him utterly. But we do not know where to find them or if they still exist (my grandfather's house was flooded by the Wolastoq one spring). Were they ever written at all?

*

Run.

*

Was shame as destructive to my father as it was to me? Can righteous pain be released by turning injury into an opportunity to understand?

*

The signs were cut or burnt into the body and advertised that the bearer was a slave, a criminal, or a traitor—a blemished person, ritually polluted, to be avoided, especially in public places.

*

My father: *Shit under my feet. Shit under my feet. Shit under my feet.* He meant me. The shit, me. The feet, his. The most intense levying of shame came when I tried to be good—which was, realistically speaking, all of the time—but my father was operating under the mistaken impression that I was bad. That shame need not be rational is the system's great secret. It need only be the household's dominant affect. Once installed, the child will be adequately trained. *Shit under my feet. Shit under my feet. Shit under my feet.*

*

Run.

*

Shame is the foundation on which all oppression operates. Humans need to be taught that they or others are bad, and the most apt pupils, the ones who are the most receptive to this idea, have been convinced of the natural correctness of the concept as children. This tragedy unfolds in billions of lives that think *I have always been bad. I will always be bad.* To make someone invalidate themselves is easy. I urge you to resist this, develop an awareness of the trick if you can. Knowing might save you, meaning you will be able to save yourself. There is no escaping, only surveying scorched earth. In the end, the shamers shame themselves.

*

Let me tell you something good because I need to believe that there *was* good. In the 1970s, my father was employed by the Emergency Measures Organization of the Province of New Brunswick. Whenever a community faced some kind of disaster, it was his job to swoop in for the rescue as the rugged, rough, and impulsive hero. One spring, the Saint John River Valley flooded particularly badly in the Sheffield area and my father, who was helping ferry stranded families to dry land, encountered a drowning man. He fished the man, named Gordon Upton, out of the water and literally saved his life, an event that made the local paper. Upton, whose barge capsized, is quoted in the May 1, 1979, edition of *The Daily Gleaner* (headline: "Man Falls Into Icy Flood Waters") as follows: "My hands were starting to get tight and I was only holding on with one of them… a few minutes later and I would have been gone."

The Daily Gleaner, Tuesday, May 1, 1979 3

Man Falls Into Icy Flood Waters

—He Was Rescued Minutes Later

By GAIL DUGAS
Staff Writer

A man fell into the near-freezing waters of the swollen St. John River yesterday while attempting to secure his small boat and barge against a river run amuck.

Gordon Upton, of Lower St. Mary's was hauled minutes later from the water by Doug Neilson of the Emergency Measures Organization who was patrolling the river. Mr. Upton fell into the river approximately 700 feet from shore when the engine on his boat broke down and the wieght of the barge capsized the smaller boat, pulling it under.

RESCUER AND RESCUED — Doug Neilson, left, of the Emergency Measures Organization, takes a break at a Salvation Army Kitchen following his rescue of Gordon Upton, right of Lower St. Mary's yesterday on the St. John River. Mr. Upton's small boat capsized on the swollen river and Mr. Neilson rescued him minutes later.

(Louella Billings Photo

"My hands were starting to get tight and I was only holding on with one of them," said Mr. Upton. "A few minutes and I would have been gone." He could only shake his head despairingly when asked about the lost boat.

A mechanic with a history of coronary problems, Mr. Upton owns an automotive shop in Lower St. Mary's. He said he will not try to recover his loss.

Besides Mr. Nielsen on the EMO boat there was also a ham radio operator and a Daily Gleaner reporter and photographer who were returning from a trip down river after viewing flood ravages on beef and dairy herds.

Approximately 300 cattle were moved to higher ground while 600-700 head remained on the highest ground on their respective farms with the hope predictions by flood specialists that the waters had crested and were beginning to subside, were correct.

Mr. Neilson attempted to secure the uninsured craft which had an estimated value of $3,800. After realizing the capsized craft could not be resurfaced, a call for help was put into the EMO headquarters. After a 25-minute wait and no visible help on the way, Mr. Neilson—concerned for the safety of his passengers and tilting boat—cut the rope loose and let the craft sink.

A request for help at the outset of the incident from radio operator Bob Abbott brought a promise from EMO headquarters that a department of natural resources boat would be on the scene "in minutes". Twenty-five minutes later, headquarters could neither report the location of the department's boat nor could they confirm the position of the craft in distress.

When fears for the safety of the passengers in the EMO craft grew, Mr. Neilson gave the order to let the craft go and his actions were radioed into the EMO headquarters.

"Nothing ventured, nothing gained," came the voice back from EMO.

Upton had a family, a wife and two little girls. In contrast with my father, I am no hero. I am a workaday clinic physician. My saving is of the slow variety, coming in the form of convincing someone to stop smoking by moving them along the stages of change model, or improving their mental health through eclectic therapy, reducing misery by a fraction each day. To save a life as my father did also requires experience and knowledge: the ability to navigate and operate a boat, strength to pluck and pull a drowning man into the hold. Doug's two inner resources were Resolve and Will, the latter quality baked into his first name: William. Mine is Care, but my name will always slant rhyme with shame.

*

Many theorists suggest that in addition to shame and guilt being related to individual variation they are also influenced by the parent-child relationship. Research additionally suggests that authoritarian, dysfunctional, critical/perfectionist focused and neglectful parenting styles link to shame. More specifically, parenting is shame-inducing when it engenders a global negative self-attribution either directly through criticism of the essential characteristics of the child or indirectly through emotional expressions that signal disgust or contempt.

*

YOU ARE SHIT, SHIT, YOU ARE SHIT, WORTHLESS SHIT, USELESS, BROKEN, NOTHING.

*

Stigma ensures we cannot hide the scandal of ourselves. Shame is an emotional response to the dilemma of difference.

*

More secret knowledge. My sister tells me of the ripples that spread in our family when I asked my aunt what it was like for my father when he was young. It turned out my uncle—Doug's younger brother—was given a copy of my aunt's letter before it was sent to me. My uncle told my sister that it was a whitewash, that my father was "given" to a neighbour farmer as a dayworker because he didn't get along with his father. The neighbour was a "boozer." When I heard this, I felt tightness in my neck, a strangling accusation hesitating for just a moment before I refused to swallow. *Who, here, is the failure?* I asked, my mind strangling an imaginary picture of my son with a hoe, standing in a cornfield, not knowing what to do, the picture replaced with an old image of me, standing in a young cornfield, barely learning what to do.

*

Later, in Christian times, two layers of metaphor were added [to stigma]: the first referred to bodily signs of holy grace that took the form of eruptive blossoms on the skin; the second, a medical allusion to this religious allusion, referred to bodily signs of physical disorder.

*

As fast as my little body can carry sticks, I carry sticks. As fast as a child can stack wood, I stack wood. Desperate to be useful, to be perceived as good, I do the work of a grown man. A stick falls from my side of the rank and hits an oil can, overturning it onto the cement floor. Doug's face moves through its progressions, from grimness to aggrieved fury. *Boy—you do it on fucking purpose. ON FUCKING PURPOSE!*

*

Run.

*

He catches me. He catches me. I can't run fast enough. I never can.

*

One of my mother's many myths: at five years old, my father packed a suitcase and pulled it to the neighbour's house. Upon knocking on the door, he explained to the matron that he was running away. She bade him come in, offered him some milk and a snack, and called my grandfather to come and get him. My mother does not continue the story, and as I was too young to ask, not only do I not know what happened next, I also do not know why my father felt he had to run away.

*

I spread his ashes over the Wolastoq with some regrets. Why did things have to be the way they were? This essay is a metaphorical re-spreading of those ashes; or, perhaps, a spreading of the ashes of mutual fatherhood. We're failures, he and I, but of a different kind.

*

Today [shame] is widely used in something like the original literal sense but is applied more to the disgrace itself than to the bodily evidence of it.

*

What is the original literal sense of the word "crazy"? *Oxford English Dictionary*: "Full of cracks or flaws; damaged, impaired, unsound; liable to break or fall to pieces; frail, 'shaky.'" And what of "disgrace"? *OED*: "ill-fortune, defeature, mishap; also, uncomeliness, deformity." The original literal sense of stigma concerns being morally unsound. The original literal sense of "shun" from the *OED*: "to cover, hide."

*

If the mark is genuinely on the body, then there is no invisible sufferer.

*

It may also bring us closer to understanding what stigma really is—not primarily a property of individuals as many have conceptualized it to be but a humanly constructed perception, constantly in flux and legitimizing our negative responses to human differences.

*

The loud truck noise in the driveway, the quality of the way the door opens, the shuffle of the figure hitting the ground, the altered gait of his inebriated approach. His steps look heavy and when they hit the hardwood floor inside, they will finally sound heavy, the sound of too-lateness. I don't know how to explain this except as a feeling that doubles as an imperative, a saving fear that is also an action: *Run.* A few times as a child, I knew to run away based on how my father approached the front door. I knew to always sit near the front window when he was gone in case he returned in this exact way. So that I could run. So that I could get away. I knew I had to run, because if I didn't, then I would be hurt. To avert hurt: this is why we run.

*

Run.

*

From his forties to his seventies, my father claimed that he lived without regrets: "I lived my life. I did what I wanted, when I wanted, and I had a good go of 'er." After the ritual pause, he would add: "After I die, spread my ashes from the Burton Bridge." He spoke casually, with a note of satisfaction. His ashes, though, still ran away on the wind.

GOFFMAN AND ME

Some nights, I dream of Goffman. We're at a diner, sharing a coffee and staring out onto a winter street. It's impossibly late—cars pass occasionally, as if to signal that time is really elapsing. Otherwise, who would know that time hadn't stopped out there, the world clutched in trauma chronology and holding its breath. Though visibility is good, no one walks towards the diner. No one feels the need to be outside. Inside, it's just me, Goffman, and two cups of coffee resting in circular grooves on saucers. Mine with cream, black for Goffman.

*

The shirt's thin weave of polyester cannot absorb all my father's sweat, nor can I reach the pedals. My legs hang in the air. My job: to steer the azure Cordoba along the winding backroads of southeast New Brunswick. Doug's too drunk to steer but not too drunk to know how fast we are going—a sensory curiosity of the intoxicated mind. With each oncoming car, I veer to the right, too far onto the thin breakdown. *It's time you learned anyway*, he says. *I was driving a tractor when I was your age.* In the confection of child entertainment, a kid driving a car is positive, a fantasy. Right? I am eight years old.

*

Our conversation is always the same. I want to know how Goffman survived his studies of stigma. In response, Goffman turns to the street and reflects for a moment, then offers this response: *I'm like that street, braced for a disaster. I survived, I suppose, because I held my breath the right way, perfectly. I didn't move, and so I wasn't noticed. Instead, the hazard hit the ones I love.* Goffman knows I'm barely surviving, that I've just come in from the cold into the diner. He knows that my family, like his, hasn't been spared. This fact is why we are friends and why we can talk about the same thing, night after night. Why he bothers to talk at all—otherwise he'd just sit alone in this diner. He makes time for me because we share, to different degrees, the tragedy. He listens to me describe the dreams that will come after our coffee, nightmares about my daughter's hair descending at the rate of 9.8 m/s^2, about me missing a phone call, her last one, that message saved as a red dot above a green box. All the cityscapes, the different shades of night—Goffman's been there.

*

Goffman published *Stigma: Notes on the Management of Spoiled Identity* in 1963. His wife, Angelica Schuyler Goffman, committed suicide a year later. Dmitri N. Shalin, Goffman's scholarly amanuensis, writes in "Interfacing Biography, Theory, and History: The Case of Erving Goffman" (2014) that:

> Everything we know about Erving Goffman indicates that he was averse to self-disclosure. He forbade

> his lectures to be tape-recorded, did not allow his picture to be taken, gave only two known interviews for the record, and sealed his archives before he died with the explanation that he wished to be judged based on his publications.... More than that, Goffman specifically disavowed research where scholars turn their attention to themselves.

Apparently, Goffman was renowned for saying, "Only a schmuck studies his own life."

*

I am eleven years old. My elder cousin and I sit at a kiddie table in my aunt's house, though we're far too old for it—our knees knock against the top. The Winnie the Pooh tablecloth is especially offensive. But such is convention: adults gather in their world, non-adults in theirs, and hierarchies are established within these groups by fellow members in their groups. Meaning, I'm at the bottom of mine. At the bottom of any. There's just me and him—all the other cousins are elsewhere, in on some fun. He says, *You know, my father isn't a drunk. If I had your father, I'd make him stop drinking.*

*

Goffman studied his own life, of course. If he had wished to be known for his work, then that work had a shadow side, a parallel track. Outside, a frozen street to observe and document; inside, the truth. I know better than to ask Goffman in my dream state what it is like to lose a loved one to mental illness, for his entire later work sings this song of loss. If you know how to look. If you are one of his "wise." If you are likewise. In the same vein, Goffman does not ask me how I feel. We subscribe to an etiquette. If we both were to speak to our experience, then the street would move again and we could never pretend there is a space where we need not make any address, ever. The street would move, another catastrophe come. Goffman and I, we do not want more trouble. We want to look intently, but also to never look.

*

A boy stands outside in freezing dew in Karate Kid pajamas, the arms and legs black but the torso grey, a red dragon blazing on the chest. He's shivering, staring at a black bungalow where crashes can be heard from inside. The starry night begins to fade into background, as does the forest in front and behind. The only visible thing is the threat within the house, meaning: the glass sliding door of the house's posterior, an imagined black portal in the greater blackness. The boy has no idea how long he hides near his backyard's one willow tree, its branches caressing his back, blowing over his face like lashes. The spindly brittle movement of it is the only detail giving the scene a sense of time passing, proof that the image is not static. The boy is convinced he *could* die, *will* die. *If* the door opens. Just like he would have died if he stayed in the house. He watches the door like his life depends on it—which it does, in fact. This moment stands as an emblem for the boy's later life, as if time were the background, all of it splashed around as a panorama in this scene. The message is understood, an unconscious knowledge: *My father could kill me.* So often would the boy come to think again that he might die that he developed a trick of greater speed—the greater the fear, the faster the running. But after a few hours of silence, his legs freezing, he goes back inside, stepping carefully towards his bedroom that shares a wall with his father's, vigilant to not create a sound, hypervigilant to a response. I remain eleven years old.

*

Goffman was remembered by his sister as "sensitive" and "sentimental," that "he was far more emotional than he wanted to exhibit." Angelica was nicknamed "Sky" by her friends. Stigma as a mark in the sky.

*

> "A girl. A retard. Faggot. Wimp."
>
> "Come out of your spin!" teammates would say as we dressed for hockey. "Come out of your spin!" Admittedly, I was daydreaming of any other place to be.
>
> Someone on the bench beside me began to match my mannerisms. They seemed to think I was a wheelchair-bound ape.
>
> I learned to stop singing along with pre-game music because they mimicked me.
>
> On day one at each new school, a lot of curious people. On day two, no one wanted to talk to me.
>
> "You look like an ape. You look like an ape. You look like an ape."
>
> "Yer fuckin useless, can't do anything."

"Your father is a fucking drunk."

Unsurprisingly, I hated going to hockey practice and tried to quit. One evening I hid in the basement, refusing to get in the car to go to the rink.

"You have to go!" said my mother. "You have to."

"I don't want to go."

"What, you don't like hockey anymore?"

"I do," I said.

"Well then, what is it?"

It was too embarrassing to say that I was despised by everyone I knew. I left the closet and walked up the stairs.

*

Outside, there is no weather. No rain or snow, nothing that might mark the passage of time. No suggestion that there even is a sky. Except for the buildings with their occasional lighted squares and streetlights that fail at illuminating the street, all is blackness. At enough distance, background and foreground merge. In trauma, any timestamp can be instantly brought together with another. The term is "triggering." Neither Goffman nor I need worry about sky and what comes from there. A car passes in perfect periodicity, as if the view were cast from a projector.

*

Being in public with my father means being in conversation with stigma. At any point, he might explode and cause a disturbance. Shouting. Shoving something off a counter. Ripping a dispenser from a wall. Pouring liquid out onto a floor. I was conditioned to be fearful of the social manifestations of his illness, the malignant power of it, and as I grew in age my fear complicated, became septated. Older, I feel stigma now as a mix of shame and fear. Shame for having his conditions myself; fear, therefore, for having the potential within me to be bad. Shame = I am bad; fear = I have the potential to be bad.

*

Goffman rarely talks. He doesn't want to talk. Or, if he wants to talk, he's restraining himself so as to modulate his appearance. Goffman is normative, you see, he can do that. I do the talking, and when one talks enough uninterrupted, that kind of one-sided conversation inevitably becomes akin to one between therapist and patient, or priest and supplicant. Yet in my "backstage"—I will develop this term of Goffman's later—I disbelieve. I think Goffman wants to listen, less to the words as such and moreso to them as stigmata of companionship. After facing great tragedy, there is nothing better than being with kin of understanding. As I look outside, the blackness of the background seems to consolidate further, the foreground moving closer, into greater resolution. I can see each rime of snowflake.

*

Standing in the backyard's freezing dew—not frost yet, but headed there, in just a few more weeks—means that I am observable, an objective marker of stigma. Even though night's entrenched, passing cars might expose me, which means it is important to not only hide from my father, but also from anyone else who could be watching. I need the willow to protect me from stigma, from an observer's knowledge that a young child is shivering, a fact easily connected with my father's reputation. Yet the paradox is that the urge to hide from the view of others is itself an action spurred by stigma. The willow branches that brush my back may not be willow branches. They may be the hands of someone else who notices. Or the hands of my father. Etc.

*

In *The Presentation of Self in Everyday Life* (1956), his first and most famous book, Goffman developed his dramaturgical analysis, a theory which holds that all people in social interactions are trying to avoid being embarrassed. In Goffman's account, people perform accordingly—to avoid being embarrassed—in what they say or don't, how they look or don't, and where they choose interactions to take place. (One can see with this line of thinking where his later work would go on stigma.) Goffman defines "frontstage" as *the expressive equipment of a standard kind intentionally or unwittingly employed by the individual during his performance.* He means that a person modifies their behaviour dependent upon the context they find themselves in, so as to enhance their reception. To put that in modern slang and adapt it for my purpose, Normies tend to maximize their chances for social impact, whereas autistics do not perceive a stage at all. In my experience, one can only slowly become more aware of a social environment over time, hoping to achieve an imperfect awareness that too easily lapses into automaticity, for it is exhausting to be running a paranoid surveillance program all the time. Goffman defines "backstage" as where *the performer can relax; he can drop his front, forgo speaking in his lines, and step out of character*. Backstage is where a person can let loose and feel relatively free from constraining context. Backstage is when we are alone. At first glance, Goffman's performance metaphor is simple and borrowed from other writers, most obviously Shakespeare among them; Goffman's innovation is in his total extension of the metaphor to involve all zones of human interaction, not only external but also internal. He develops metaphors called frontstage and backstage to spatially organize all human sociality and agency. But what division is possible for those without an awareness of the stage at all?

*

Disaster came early in the day, the sun still shining, and I ran out the back door to sit under an elm tree, visible from the Waasis Road. If it were blessed evening, the backyard willow would have worked, but as it was afternoon—who knows why he came home?—I needed to be undetectable to any observer inside the house. I needed to be out of view. Just a few minutes after my settling under the tree, an elderly man approaches. Balding, with tufts of white hair circling just above his ears, he says, *Hey, are you ok?* Well, no. I am not. In these situations, I am usually found crying, always shaking and shameful. *Listen, I know—you're, you're Doug's son, right?* Then I ran away again, but this time into the further forest, saved from complete lostness only by arriving at the highway. Another similar time: struggling behaviourally in junior high school, defiant, compulsively speaking to others during class. One day a gym teacher brings me into his office and tries to empathize and connect. *Of course, I know what it must be like at home, with someone like your father…* That sentence was never finished. I shoved my chair back and walked out, slamming the door behind me. Forty years since that moment, I still can't tell what was worse: terror in the house, or confirmation of stigma outside of it.

*

Originally, Goffman was staunchly anti-psychiatry. In *Asylums* (1961), he wrote that *the "mentally ill"… and mental patients distinctly suffer not from mental illness, but from contingencies* and that *the craziness or "sick behavior" claimed for the mental patient is by and large a product of the claimant's social distance from the situation that the patient is in and is not primarily a product of mental illness.* Embarrassed (ironically) by Goffman's gauche denial of biomedical reality, some scholars wish to complicate Goffman's views and obfuscate the fact that he denied an organic truth about mental illness, that he gave biology its due in an oblique fashion. They needn't have bothered. Anyone who reads Goffman fairly will conclude that, early on, he was very biased against a biological etiology; furthermore, he mercilessly critiqued institutions tasked to deal with mental illness without offering a single meaningful alternative. Don't worry, I've talked with him about this period in his life. He's sorry for it. He was made sorry for it, for, according to Shalin, Sky was under the care of many psychiatrists during her marriage to Goffman. Further punishment: Sky made several suicide attempts in the 1950s. Eventually, in *Relations in Public: Microstudies of the Public Order* (1971), Goffman admitted that psychiatric disorders are "organic in their relevant cause." I myself agree by half.

*

In "Goffman on Mental Illness" (2013), Shalin writes that there is

> no doubt that the change in Goffman's perspective echoed his tragedy. On April 27, 1964, Schuyler Goffman committed suicide by jumping off the Richmond-San Rafael Bridge (Oakland Tribune, 1964). Several symptoms mentioned in [his essay "The Insanity of Place"] strike the reader as highly specific, even idiosyncratic, yet nearly perfectly aligned with the Goffman's family situation as reported by numerous witnesses who recall Schuyler's highly emotional reaction to the Kennedy assassination, obsession with national politics, preoccupation with philanthropic ventures, references to her great ancestors, eagerness to invite coworkers to family gatherings, and so on.

Biocriticism is untrustworthy. Trust the tale and not the teller—but what if the tale is about the teller? There is something lurid in pointing to Goffman's great loss, something truly unknowable, a variable I must mathematically assign as *x* for it is too confident to explain with certainty and exactitude as "the death of Sky." I hang *x* in the frame of Goffman's early work. As if Goffman's life were a simple fable. But it is this elegance that gives Goffman's story its power, the stakes of his academic stance granting gravitas. Look—the distinguished, stoical old man at the diner. What would we both, Goffman and me, give to get our loves restored?

*

In 1963, a year before she dies, Sky Goffman writes a letter to a friend: *For a variety of reasons, I am currently higher than a kite despite or maybe because of a new bout of arm trouble. Sometimes I think oh well, this is just the manic phase; occasionally I think my god, maybe a non-depressive life is possible. (You know, I feel I've never adequately expressed to you how much I owe you and Addie for the general shoring up and salvage work, especially that first grim winter out here. I know one isn't supposed to say these things—especially if in any way affiliated with one E. Goffman—but I often think it).*

*

It is said that autistics have "black-and-white thinking." Though this distinction applies mainly to morality, I believe it also applies to perception. For me, scenes possess a flat depth. There is what is immediately in front of me, as if a flat screen; then there is what is beyond, a larger screen. Items are compressed in space in two categories, near and far. Goffman's dramaturgical analysis is germane here. For the normative, how they should act to get what they want is up front for them; what they actually want and how they truly feel is in back. Such a division has contiguity with my depth perception. Goffman and me in the diner, we see sky and buildings as blackness on a greater blackness. Elements of background fuse with other elements to form homogeneous blackness; as for foreground, there is just enough refreshing detail to reassure us that our place is real, but also that it, like the background, remains held. The governor of time is trauma, crushing the past, present, and future into a single moment, and this chamber I share with Goffman is the result of that singularity. Frontstage and backstage are separated by a thin membrane, and Goffman and I are squeezed somewhere in there. If both stages are extant, then what does Goffman want as part of his front, and how does he feel as part of his back? What do I want from Goffman, how do I feel? As ever: what to feel, how to feel?

*

Who knows how long we've sat here? When time doesn't pass, how long is how long? It's not as if we have anywhere to go. Here is enough, less sanctuary than waystation. Even *I've* stopped talking, preferring to watch the snow sit and glow on the ground, little streets of it pressing against the curb. *What I want is impossible, I know this. Yet I can't stop wanting it. I want Sky back. I want to go back in time and save her. My whole life points backward.* I would of course grant him his wish if I could, but mirroring his own foolish wish, I cannot become a granter of wishes. Rather than judge him for treating Sky poorly, for denying the reality of her illness – who knows if that is so? – I conduct my own time travel, retreating backstage to where my daughter descends slowly, as if falling through amber. What about all the things I didn't say, the things I should have said, the things I should have done? The care not taken?

*

In *The Savage God*, published in 1971, seven years after the death of Goffman's Sky, Al Alvarez offers what the *New York Times* called "a long, brooding, melodramatic meditation on suicide." A main focus of the book is the last days of one of the twentieth century's major poets, Sylvia Plath, who in 1963 stuck her head in a gas oven as her two children slept, but only after having prepared breakfast for them. For a general reader, Alvarez's version of the tale is compelling yet respectful. But all readers are not general. One reader, Plath's ex-husband Ted Hughes, had had to live past the further death of his mistress, Assia Wevill, who, like Plath, also died by gas oven in 1969, though in this case with the escalation of killing little Shura, the couple's daughter. The interpersonal details in this love triangle as well as their broader context in Hughes's serial infidelity are not relevant here. What is relevant is the sheer gravity of suicide, its weight and inexorability. It exists in space as a series of actions and it exists in time as always nearing closer. Hence Goffman and I, we need space hyper-realized, foreground and background. We need time as a simulacrum of time, plausibly passing, though we know it isn't. He and I are held in the dream-room. Goffman, antipsychiatry, Sky; me, genetics, offspring. We both know so well Hughes's condemnatory letter to Alvarez; we've memorized it, discussed it like scholars, as true students of our own lives. I quote it to him: *[H]istory tries to repeat itself even without human help, it didn't occur to you that her children are left with an even more dangerous situation than hers & with all her vulnerabilities.* I pause, as I always do, and wait for Goffman's responsorial psalm. *Electrodes in her children's brains.* Then I intone the second quote: *In a real way, you have robbed them of her death, of any natural way of dealing with her death. This will add up through every year they live.* And Goffman responds while staring out the window, *Electrodes in her children's brains.* Of course, Hughes was right: his son Nicholas would later hang himself. Hughes knew because he saw. As a father, he raged to protect his family from the obsessive, ghoulish focus of an insatiable public upon their mother's death, what Mark Ford in the *New York Review of Books* characterized as "a heroic, morally persuasive, dignified, but always doomed war." And yet I say it was not Hughes's war that was doomed. It was his children who were doomed. Hughes was doomed to fight the war. Hughes knew the doom to come, and who truly knows what would have happened to his children should he not have fought it? Furthermore, Hughes was right to hate Alvarez thereafter. Alvarez had visited the couple in their flat. He was a guest. For any father, it is as if a sly thief had stolen something precious, and then resold it as fentanyl to the father's children so that they could die too.

*

The picture I have in my mind of my father's childhood is nightmarish, the worst version possible. I know it to be an exaggeration, but of course it has to be—he was an exaggeration, a caricature, charming when he wanted something, instrumental to the core, with cyclic periods of chaotic destruction. A second version consisting of stitched-together accounts told by others features terrifying vignettes alternating with instances where he helped someone tremendously. In this second version, a more complicated man emerges. Years ago, I wrote to my aunt, my father's elder sister, for a narrative about what it was like for my father as a child. Her response sat unopened on my desk for over three years, emanating the power of nightmare—this, even though I knew my aunt would provide a sanitized version, a Beaver Cleaver rural idyll, scenes of fields and tractors and 4-H meetings. One day, I open it and encounter what I expect to find. Somehow, though, this met expectation is worse than the terror I secretly hoped would be there. For if the letter described terrible things being done to him, then I could forgive him for the terrible things done to me. That there exists this third, fairy-tale version, one that refuses to engage with difficulty because of stigma, means that I must merge my account with those of the others in order to dial down the nightmare. Nevertheless, it is all nightmare—the feeling overwhelms recollection of quiet and calm moments, data points rejected in order to prove the hypothesis.

*

We're doing the Hughes Letter Seminar again. *But you say much more than I do*, Goffman says. *Though you know.* I do know—this whole essay is about suicide as a force that coheres around difference and disability, how life proceeds as if such people should be extinguished. And in the case of the children who follow their parents, that they follow completely. Why, then, do I write that which could call what I fear into being? I write as an attempt at anti-gravity, less for my own survival as testament and more so that my children can read of living *with* illness and strangeness; I write so that these fractured accounts might suggest to them that every second was enough, that my love for them was enough. That they were enough for me; that they are enough for themselves. If I live, then there will be my example and person to push against risk. If I die, then perhaps what I have written will be enough to keep them safe, enough to disabuse them of the death-romance of poets, even as the data point, the end point, sings to them as possibility.

*

My father never spoke about his work to me, about what it was like for him as a man who never finished high school to go in a stupid suit every day to an office where he had to talk to college-educated people. I only know that he often didn't make it in to work; whenever there was a professional development day at school, he would stay at home and make life difficult for me. As a doctor, I routinely feel impostor syndrome; that I don't know enough, that I'm incompetent. How did my father feel, as a civil servant with a secretary who could spell adequately—meaning far better than he could? How hard was it for him to live a life where he had to pass? He could pass, mostly, depending on the day. But what if it wasn't one of those days? And even if it was, he still had to think about not passing. Did he pick the days he went to work so he could pass better?

*

Stereotyping is frequently tied to the need for self-enhancement. People with low self-esteem are more likely to identify and maintain negative stereotypes about members of stigmatized groups; such people are more negative in general.

*

On the news, another school shooting in the USA, another dozen or so dead. The white male—almost always a white male—has a history of mental health issues. The feeling inaugurates in my neck, a combination of breathless running and choking that mounts until I actually can't breathe, as if the feeling were a flag and asphyxia the destination. The hack reporter says, *He has a history of mental health issues, Julie, but that's all we know at this time from his Facebook account. He had a history of harassing women, and may have been on medication. We're calling the family home now, but no one is answering. This is fast-breaking news. Twelve dead and several more injured…* Accursed network, please don't show the shooter's face. Don't show me the yearbook photograph with the flat gaze, the always-knew-it'd-be-you face, the killer-psycho-nothing-registers-face. Because that's my face, you're showing my kind of face, stop showing my face!

*

In many respects, we remind you of you, and you do not like being us.

*

From the perspective of cognitive psychology, when people find it necessary or beneficial to perceive the fundamental similarities they share with stigmatized people rather than the differences, we will see the beginnings of a real elimination of stigma.

*

Odd that we're friends. Goffman was such a good explicator of the mechanisms of stigma because he himself was entirely a creature of it. According to Gary Marx, one of his former students, he *persisted in talking about "gimps,"* even though *[t]here was a badly crippled woman in the class.* The student adds that there was also a student with *a severe stuttering problem. This did not prevent her from asking questions. Acting as if she was not present, Goffman offered material... about how stutterers managed (e.g., by taking jobs as night watchmen).* Perhaps his presence here in the diner is not only companionship for me, as created by me, but a mutuality. Maybe Goffman feels like a penance of silence is required, but not one conducted in solitude. Maybe he's been waiting to hear me speak of this the whole time. *Goffman,* I say to get his attention, which, lately, has been focused on staring at the outer darkness. He doesn't turn his head, but I go on anyway. *I never knew this for decades, but all the people that were kind to me, patient, the few I could call my friends—every one of them were exceptionally confident in themselves. And this was the very attraction they held to me, lacking such confidence.* Goffman turns his head to me. I have his attention. *And what,* he asks, *did they say to you?* Me: *They mostly listened, as I recall.* Goffman, who has never smiled, not once since we've been here, betrays the smallest trace of a smirk as he turns back to the blackness.

SECTION TWO:

DIFFERENCE

DIAGNOSIS DAY

In a few minutes, I'll meet Dr. Vicki Nolan, clinical psychologist, for an assessment regarding possible autism. In my hand is my usual order, a Starbucks venti dark roast with room for cream. I sit in a predictable spot (as far away from people as possible). All the usual conditions apply, and they are vast. Life is an unusual condition, but if I perform the same routines, I will make it through the day intact. I am armoured with this technology of the self.

Ask yourself: how many routines are part of your day that you don't even notice? Tooth brushing. Shower. Shave. Dry. Dress. Drive. Coffee. For my son, a pictogram helps him with routines. Mine are always front of mind. If they are not front of mind, then I cannot reassure myself that they are there, that they have been completed, or will be completed.

Repetition is in and of my mind, not as obsession or compulsion but rigid routine. Over and over and over and over and over again. A routine: I arrive two hours early for an appointment that starts at 9:30 a.m.

I don't know if I have autism, am autistic—I am not invested overmuch in language games—but because I've suspected the diagnosis since I started graduate work in disability studies, I've finally decided to disregard my internalized stigma. I'm curious. So many in this life seek a metanarrative as Explanation for All Things. I'm looking for a reason for isolation, for preferring it, for why people react to me like I emit the keen of a dentist's drill. Why no one wanted to play with me as a child; why I have few friends. Why I still don't know exactly how to be a friend. I know what friendship means in the abstract, but not how to enact it.

This appointment has taken me over a year to get. But I'm here. Another routine: I always do the things I say I will do. The pattern of repetition, re-wording in the mind: what to feel, how to feel, what to feel, how to feel, what to feel, how to feel, what to feel, how to feel, what to feel, how to feel, what to feel, how—

My mother once said she had me take an assessment before I started elementary school. I don't remember this, even though I remember most things—as you will see.

Numbers? No, I can forget numbers. Conversations I remember verbatim. I'm the best lie detector ever invented if one had all the time in the world. I will never forget what's said. Images? Less so because I retain them in the proxy of words. I think in terms of signifiers, not the signified. My one category weakness in words is people's names. I recite names repeatedly, so I don't feel self-conscious about saying them, in which case I won't utter them at all in public. If I don't say them in person, I'm cursed to not remember them. This is the double bind.

I remember the intake school sign-up session I attended with my mother, even though I don't remember the testing. There, Mrs. Logue and Mrs. Momborquette sat at a card table in the gym, processing applications. A near sawdust-dry elementary gym next to the army base, surrounded by Private Military Quarters (PMQs) of only two hues, off-white and green—childhood as nausea's palette.

Mrs. Momborquette. Her husband was named Joe. Was he a member of parliament? Or MLA? MLA. Conservative. Conservative, because my father liked him. Mrs. Momborquette, who I never spoke to again, fated to never have her as a teacher. My teacher, old Logue, seemed to decay each day, her face cracking in a powdery foundation, white fault lines against a green chalkboard. Dust against the chalkboard, either from her face or from the chalk erasers, *clap clap*, the dust motes in the summer light creating an off-white shimmer against the green. Nausea. Nausea's palette.

I don't remember the process for being assessed as "gifted," a circumstance which is odd considering my otherwise preternatural powers of recall. Yet I remember my mother telling me much later in life, *You were identified as gifted, but I wanted you in the regular classes so that you could be more social.* She told me this a year before she died, writing out the words in her block script on a piece of paper because an endotracheal tube was lodged in her throat.

The focus then was, of course, not on me, but rather on her, on some desperate way to right the ship, her ship, to keep it from going down. After it sank, I was left with questions I had to work out myself. Questions that can no longer be answered, like: what did it mean to be "gifted?" Did it mean "retarded?" Like: what did you think of me as a child,

Mom? You must have noticed that I was different. Were you ashamed of me?

I was ashamed of myself. I was taught to be ashamed.

The only other conversation I had with my mother about my strangeness occurred during a trip back to New Brunswick when I was thirty-five years old and was conducted in the presence of a friend I brought to a poetry festival in Fredericton. I was talking to my friend about what it was like in Oromocto years ago. My mother asked innocuously, *And what was it like for you in school?*

I answered the question in my usual detailed way. I said, *I was bullied every day of my life. I didn't know how to play with other kids when I was younger and still don't have much of an idea of how to be comfortable around people, though I'm getting better. I was so sad as a child. I didn't know what to say or do. I didn't have any skills or know how to ask for help. So, I just read books, lots of books, which helped a lot.* She said nothing in response. What did she think?

Looking back at what I said to my mother, I see I was conceptualizing a mental illness discourse. I thought maybe I had "social anxiety." If I could rephrase things to her today, my answer would mention an inability to engage in *social reciprocity*. But I'm only left with questions. Staving off the uncertainty are routines.

A memory keeps coming back every week or so: I'm twelve years old. Mom picks me up after a summer camp held at Yoho Scout Reserve. It went poorly (everything I did with other people went poorly). For three days, I faced bullying and shaming by more socially adept boys in a million little ways that don't matter, that by then were too familiar, even intimate. That's not important. That we know how to treat one another terribly is not essential, but the following conversation with my mom reproduced faithfully in a dream, that's what matters now. *So, how did the camp go, Shane?* my mother asks. *Did you have a good time?* The Scouts had just completed a game in which we hid in a defined area, and an older scout had to find us. Because I was the last found, because I had the instinct to find the best places to hide (not only an instinct, but training, a survival strategy), and I was notable for something other than being strange, I was happy. *Yes*, I said with excitement. My mother said, *Really? Well, I didn't sign you up for the next camp, but I'll do that because you enjoyed it. I'm so glad!* Me: *Well, actually, I'm not sure. I mean, it was kind of bad too.* Mom: *Look. I'm trying to find out what you like. Did you like it or not?* I wanted to please her, and I didn't know what to say about the bullying. *I liked it*, I decided. *Yes.*

At the next camp, I didn't win anything. Bullying was duly delivered.

*

In Grade 8, I became the pet project of Alex de la Rosa, a Normie who lived in Deer Park, a semi-detached community just down the street from me. You could say I got socially adopted out to him, or he Normie Eyed the Weird Guy.

We were the same age. Similarities stop there. Alex was into guns and weights and hated his parents; he was also socially adept, dressed well, and even had a girlfriend. I have no idea why he befriended me. Maybe there are a few vulnerable souls you can remake in your image?

He taught me that the sweatpants I wore to school every day needed to be replaced with a variety of jeans and dress pants. He forced me to get regular haircuts. He introduced me to his friends, the cool kids in school—people so far out of my orbit they weren't even aware of my existence. Kids who got drunk and vomited in pits. He tried to teach me what to say and do around girls, but that was hopeless.

We stayed friends for six months. He was incredibly cruel, mirroring my behaviour so that I became more socialized. He thought mockery was the way to self-improvement. *Shane, do you think staring at people is a quality attribute? Shane, are you in there? Whoo-hoo, earth to Shane, earth to Shane? Look me in the eyes, dude. I'm over here. My eyes, dude. Eyes, dude. Eyes.*

At a school sock hop near the end of the year. I see Alex walking around the gym and try to get his attention, saying *Hi* through Belinda Carlisle's blaring, "Baby, Leave a Light on for Me." Alex runs away, dodging people as they walk around the gym. I figure it's a game and chase him for a couple of revolutions until he turns around and shows me his fists, waving them in front of my face. I walk away from the gym and back to homeroom, where I sit at my desk and stare out the window at a PMQ. That was the end of our friendship and the socialization project. It took someone showing me their fists for me to get the picture.

*

After a relatively free-flowing interview, Dr. Nolan asks me standardized questions used to diagnose adults with autism. I answer with ambivalence—my usual routine. Am I malingering? My wife isn't sure I'm on the spectrum.

When I told a friend I would be getting assessed, he said, *Don't you think this is just normal stuff? I don't like to be around people either*. The whole time I'm with Dr. Nolan, I can't help but think that I'm like everyone else, that I shouldn't be here.

Wait.

This essay isn't about why I do or don't have autism. It's not a proof. I'm not here to perform, to satisfy diagnostic criteria. This essay is about a feeling. An enormous feeling.

Wait.

You need to read some things before you'll understand. Then you will know the feeling that I mean. Or maybe there's something wrong with you?

*

My brother Corey had friends. I sometimes played with them because they needed another body in ball hockey, where three is more fun than two, and four is way better than three. I didn't know it then, but watching my brother interact with his friends made friendship possible for me many years later. Like everyone else, they understood that I was strange, but because I was Corey's brother and they needed a third or fourth, I was permitted to play. Best of all, because my brother didn't despise me like the bullies did, and because he modelled kindness to his friends, they were in turn disposed to be kind to me.

In school, no one was kind to me. Distracted by sound, overwhelmed by light, wearing the same clothes day after day, indescribably (but quietly) angry when routines were violated, at sea when there was no structure or rules to engage in discussion and then—whoosh. Bully pulled my pants down, and the other kids laughed.

In medical school, I didn't look or talk like everyone else. My speech was complex, layered, and recursive; my face didn't show any emotion except for anger. Consequently, I was demonized as a bad student, a problem person. A dean once told me, *You are not capable of change.*

A fatherly plastic surgeon from Saint John once told me over a facial flap about a successful surgical technique: *If you do the same thing the same way each time, you will get the same result.* He offered this as a prescription for excellence. His technique was great because he duplicated routine. I felt as if I was in the presence of the gospel. Because he was a kind man, maybe even a wise one, I decided to use this statement to explain all my life's routines, including those that needed to be changed.

Do you need evidence? Do you wish to verify the story? Do you need proof?

*

I'm eight years old, at home, shitting on the toilet. The bathroom door is open. My father walks by and asks, *What are you doing?* I respond, *I'm using the bathroom.* He says, *When you use the bathroom, you should always close the door.* Then he closes it for me. He doesn't scream. He doesn't slam. He just speaks in a neutral voice. I always close the door after that. Routine perfected.

I'm twelve years old, and I'm wearing a belt. But it's not on right. In the living room, my father says, *Why is your belt on like that?* I respond, *On like what?* Father: *You should have your belt in line with the zipper and buttons on your shirt so that everything's straight. And it should go through all the pant loops.* I look down, and the belt's off to the side. Functionally, it works; but aesthetically, it seems like I've not put it on properly. But I don't know what my father means, not really (there is always that particular "but." The normal "but." What is "normal?") He stands, walks toward me, and takes the belt out. Then he carefully puts it back on my waist, threading it through all the loops and tightening it in alignment. When he's done, I must admit—it does work better. I always put a belt on properly after that. Routine perfected.

Perhaps twice a month, my wife will say: *Your shirt's inside out.* Most of the time, she tells me in the morning. Sometimes, though, she only notices at night. Evading her detection system, I'll make it to work where a patient will tell me that the shirt is on inside out, or I'll notice myself on a virtual appointment screen. In Newfoundland, this happened so often that nurses told me a piece of folklore: that I had to wear the shirt inside-out for the rest of the day to placate the ghosts who would be angry if I were to turn the shirt right side round.

Reader, I feel like I am about to disclose a secret to all life, as such a secret was given to me (forgive the biblical intonation, but I truly believe I am about to tell you something important). What I will tell you is a *secret*, and if you do it too, then perhaps in time, with many repetitions, you'll realize just how great a secret it is.

My father, for some reason—he must have been cued for a reason—appears in front of my bedroom door, which is directly across from the bathroom. He's draped in a towel, and he's still wet. Through a beatific grin, he says, *There is nothing better than getting under the warm water and taking a shower. Whenever you're sick, you can just get under the shower and you'll feel better. It will change you. You'll get clean, and even if you're still sick, at least you're clean and sick.* After that, I shower every day and have learned his great truth. Routine perfected.

Is this also evidence? In my first year of medical school, away from home for the first time and living with an older couple on Shirley Street, I sometimes showered three times a day. I liked how the water felt. Routine perfected.

In 2012, during my MFA, I worked with an esteemed writer who had written several books on plot. There aren't many Canadian writers who have written books on plot, let alone *multiple* books. I chose to study under the writer because my stories didn't have any. During the mentorship, it became apparent that I may never, ever, understand how to create plot. *It's probably just a mental block*, he said. *You can analyze plot, but you can't write it for some reason. Helluva sentence writer you are. It'll come. Give it time.* I sat down and tried to figure it out. I wrote a long essay titled "What Does Anybody Want?" about how I couldn't understand people's motivations generally, how desire is a constant mystery. No one has read it because I've kept it in a drawer. Who would understand an essay about a writer whose plot was to understand plot? What would people think I wanted?

To be understood.

The famous writer's advice: *figure out what your character wants and constantly delay them from getting it.* How does anyone write a plot if they don't know what someone wants? Plus, desire is more than knowing what someone wants. It is being able to recognize desire in other people. I want to know what other people want.

*

Dr. Nolan asks, *Tell me how you feel a feeling in your body, physically.* Me: *I don't feel things in my body like that. Emotions aren't in my body.* As I'm talking, I'm wondering what my face looks like. This is a remarkable notion—a thought I've seldom had. Nolan: *They're not?* Me: *No. They're in my consciousness.* Nolan: *No sensations, though, you're sure?* Me: *No. Should there be? Wait.* Dr. Nolan waits, and I think of a Dilbert cartoon where a tech nerd has a thought bubble over his head with one word: PROCESSING. *Wait,* I say again. *There is one feeling, yes, that's in my body. It's sadness. I feel sadness in my body. It's a heaviness on my chest as if I can't breathe. Not short of breath, just that I can't breathe.* Sadness is not being able to breathe. *That's good!* she says.

*

Facial expression test time by way of flash cards. I figure I'll fail. Guess the eye expressions? FAIL. Explain a weird children's story that has no linear narrative. FAIL. Make shapes with blocks? FAIL. At the end of the day, Dr. Nolan says she'll review the information, and we'll meet again for a feedback session. Janet must fill out some collateral questionnaires, and I say sure. Dr. Nolan doesn't say FAIL. Though I say FAIL.

*

Janet asks at the dinner table, *Are you excited about your follow-up appointment tomorrow*? I respond, *I'm not invested in the outcome. Whatever happens, that's fine.* My son Kaz's mouth overfloweth with french fries. Inside, a voice: *What else could make sense?* A beat later: *You're not normal. Isn't that enough? To be undifferentiated and leave it at that? What are you really hoping for?* A beat later: *Are you faking it?* A beat later: *You're abnormal, c'mon, you're just fucking weird.* A beat later: *You're faking it.* A beat later, I see a version of myself at eight years old, sitting impassively at a wooden school desk. In an hour, I'll head out on the playground where I will be alone. A beat later, I mentally say something back to the bullying voice: *Tell the little kid that.* I think the little kid will kick Voice's ass.

*

Routine. Repetition. I'm in Starbucks two hours early for a follow-up appointment scheduled at noon. Venti coffee, dark roast with cream. I don't care if I have autism. I don't care if I don't. I'm not invested in the outcome either way. I don't know what to feel. Everyone feels this way sometimes, right? That they don't know what to feel? Or how to feel?

You scored 98 percent on verbal reasoning, Dr. Nolan says, *which I don't think will be a surprise. That's very high. But your nonverbal reasoning score is average. Then this test corroborates, and that test is suggestive, and this test and that test and…*

The little boy from forty years ago: maybe you ended up in family medicine because you needed to land in an accommodating workplace environment with a predictable load and a stable schedule that involves interacting with only one other person at a time. The little boy from forty years ago: I want to do work with the Physicians Health Program of Ontario and the Canadian Medical Protective Agency around autism, especially around professionalism. I want to educate the professional associations that autistic people need accommodations and won't respond to therapeutic regimes for addiction and mood disorders as neurotypical people do.

Dr. Nolan, do you actually help doctors like me? Do you work with them, support them? Help them see themselves and learn how to better integrate into their environments? Do you help the environments work with them? I ask. She responds, *I do. It's usually after the person has gotten into some disciplinary trouble, so I'd like things to start earlier, but I've been doing this for a few years now.*

Suddenly, I know what to feel. I don't need the distillation of poetry or the writing process to know what to feel. Not right now, not like usual. Sadness—no, wait. Not that. Grief? *Grief.* The anguish of being characterized as bad, bad for so many years, all the external badness served up as my medicine, as my dose to take—I feel it in my chest. I feel it coming down all at once, grief to be exorcized in the form of breath, grief as an immense relief. I say, *I'm so glad that there is help now, that people like me can get help, that they don't have to be bad.*

The little boy from forty years ago moves a bit closer into the room.

SPOON UNDER THE TABLE

Let's start with the lie: what Shane "has" is "invisible" to you. Because I lack a malformed or missing limb, a wheelchair, tracheostomy, or oxygen tank, I have no objective proof of disability.

In *The Disability Studies Reader*, Lerita Coleman Brown writes, *Physical abnormalities, for example, may be the most severely stigmatized differences because they are physically salient, represent some deficiency or distortion in the bodily form, and in most cases are unalterable.* Yet my alterity is unalterable, and to be on a locked psychiatric ward is to have no agency in bodily form.

Understand the paradox: the most severely stigmatized difference is the kind one doesn't acknowledge. To be removed from the world is the most extreme kind of invisibility. The knowledge derived from my body is that affect is visible in the world, and if not as a substance, then in terms of its effects. For example, if I showed you specific configurations of my father's face, you would come closer to understanding what I mean. You would know something was wrong. If I put you in his presence when he was compelled to make such faces, you would come even closer to understanding.

Meet Doug. Look first, and only then pronounce upon invisibility: *Shit under my feet. Shit under my fucking feet!* I had said something wrong, done something wrong. Or, according to variation, I had not said or done anything. That's the carousel, reversing its spin to keep this rider clutching the horse's reins. Which was it? No time to guess, only to watch, which is a kind of holding on. Doug's face contorts, transforms—the eyes jut forward past the lips and the cheeks ascend to the ceiling. *You do it on FUCKING PURPOSE.* His lips press, turn inward and retract into liplessness. His teeth expose, making his skull a foreboding of death. *My* death. What did I do, though? What didn't I do? I can't remember. I never know. Questions like these aren't helpful except as a warning. Asking them isn't useful except perhaps a premonition for my feet to move. My father's face rematerializes into an impending disaster signal, and, as per all acts of God, one can die from the searing truth. Detecting the warning means that I'm still within reach, still rag-doll-able. Doug declares his intent to strike when his masseters clench, though by that point, my feet have usually acted on the warning already. Should have.

Is what transforms my father invisible? I describe a negative radiance, a passionate and inexhaustible malevolence. Doug's eyes become big as his rage reaches better-to-eat-you-with proportions, a family relation come unto wolf. Then, and always, these final countdown words are spoken in a frighteningly neutral voice: *You waste my time.* Oh, God. His utterance marks the penultimate part of the death sequence. It means I am out of time. It means—*run.* Think of this poor child running to save his life whenever someone says, "invisible disability."

Why is my turbulent, impeded, stigmatized negotiation of the world designated as "invisible"? Simple. If the "invisible" idea is deemed applicable, if it can be put in play, the disabled instantly become a successfully rendered desire of ableist society—to *be* invisible. To disappear. To not be heard from. We invisibles are like the poor that society prefers not to see wading through its intersections but are now like the same poor that neoliberalism blames as lacking resilience. It is the not-so-secret wish of society for me to remain invisible as a citizen and sufferer. I am easier to manage as a compromised paradox: Depending on the situation, my "active" illness—meaning I am impaired in thought and mood—is wielded as justification for further relegations to a margin. To you, I might seem irritable, even angry, or sullen. I might sit in a torpor, unable to process more than a single aural stimulus. I must stand at certain points; other times, I need to walk. Such deviance is both proof and reason to leave me alone, to offer opportunity to someone seemingly more normal, to render me *invisible.* I'm crazy, so you leave me alone, but because you leave me alone, you'll never discover I'm not crazy.

The mechanism of stigma is to create pariahs, to convert suffering into moral weakness and insult. According to this logic, invisibility is the fate of the ill, accomplished less through confrontation and more by subtly privileging those more congenial and more receptive to social approach.

Maybe this book is a visibilizing, a making manifest, a conversation by a ghost for other ghosts. This book is for the spirits and the monsters under the bed as much as it is for people treated like monsters. Maybe this essay needs a domestic object to make the lie of invisibility hit home.

Everyone holds a domestic object in particular regard, a painting or an old toy. Often these unique objects are mounted on a wall or rest on a desk, meant to be noticed. My special object, however, is not intended to be observed. By keeping the object masked by its nondescript purpose, I need not ever discuss the associated memory. In an overstuffed kitchen drawer, Goldilocks sizing applies: a small spoon sits for my son; larger spoons for my wife and daughter; a big spoon for me. Some suppers, I turn in my chair and look out the window. My neighbour's east brick wall is in view, less than two metres distant. The wall ascends enough to block both street and sky. When I return to the conversation at the dinner table, I am sometimes terrified by the spoon lying next to my plate or bowl. A doctor (whose name I didn't say out loud to remember) once told me this was a sign of trauma.

Sometimes I wonder what it was like for my father, I say. *Growing up.* Dr. Pink, my psychiatrist, asks, *In what way?* Sleepy-eyed and arch, she's like an owl snoozing in the corner of a barn until it swoops down with open talons. *Well, now that I have a son that doesn't seem to be like other kids, and having lived a life myself in which I was often told I was different, I begin to wonder just how "bad" my dad really was.* Pink: *Do you mean that you're learning to forgive him because you're learning it's not so easy to be a parent?* Me: *Not exactly, no. What happened to me as a child shouldn't have happened and I'll never agree or accept otherwise. And yet forgiveness exists in what I'm saying now and have been saying for a long time.* Pink waits. *My dad lived a life in which he was made out to be a monster, the devil; he did all sorts of insane, violent, selfish things. Then he falls off the top of a tractor-trailer and suffers a head trauma so severe that he spends over six months in hospital, learning how to take care of himself again. He gets epilepsy due to the brain scarring, and the anticonvulsants he's given also serve as mood stabilizers. Lo and behold, he was much easier to be around after that, much more reasonable. He didn't experience a total personality change or anything. He wasn't suddenly converted into an angel. He was still a difficult man. But it's like… a monster wasn't out to eat me so much anymore, you know? I could relax next to him.* Swoop: *We already covered the evidence of your father having bipolar disorder years ago. Why are you mentioning this now?* Me: *It's because I have a son. I'm worried about the world he's going to meet. I'm worried that the conditions in my house will recreate the conditions in my father's house. There's a family legend that at five years old, my dad hated home so much that he packed a bag and went to the neighbour's place and told them that he had "moved out." His father walked over and dragged him from there as he was watching television.* I realize that there are so many stories. Why couldn't I remember them before? *Another story: my dad joined the army at sixteen to get away from home.* Pink: *So?* Me: *I'm just beginning to wonder what kind of compassion he was ever shown as a young person. He must have been ill like me. But we're talking sixty years ago in a poor, rural place. The worst thing for me—worse even than the home environment—was how shunned I was as someone with difference. I can only imagine what it was like for him.* Pink lets me talk more, it's her great talent. She's returned to the rafters and I'm safe to ramble on the most obvious topic in the world—Daddy. For a man so stigmatized, how was Doug's disability invisible?

Several times a year, my father would insist that the spoon in front of him was not a spoon, or that his plate was cracked, or that there was no salt on the table. *This is not a spoon. I told you, bitch, this isn't a goddamn spoon. Not a spoon, not a fucking spoon. It's a piece of shit. You get this shit and you say it's cutlery but it's not fit for nothing. You do this on purpose. You do this on FUCKING PURPOSE.* One cue to run away from my father as fast as possible were the words "on purpose." He always said these words angrily, so I was grateful for the signal—that clue gave me time to flee. But another, more difficult cue came when he would say, calmly, *You are wasting my time.* I ran for my life when I heard those words. He bent the spoon in half as a preliminary. His arm became a scythe reaping the food off the table, shoving it to the floor. He stood, found a pot with bubbling sauce, and threw it against the wall to make a red Rorschach splotch run down the beige paint. The fridge's contents were emptied, tossed around the kitchen. In time, none of the doors in the inner part of the fridge worked and food had to be piled on a single level. But who would know? All of this occurred invisibly, meaning inside the house, away from you.

I've just dropped off my son at school, and I watch him slowly make his way up to the door amongst a press of kids. A teacher approaches. *Who are you?* she asks, forcefully. Before I can respond, she adds, *Do you have a child who attends this school?* I look around, noting about a dozen other parents also watching their children filter into the building. *Why are you asking me who I am when there so many other people doing the same thing as me?* I continue. *Is it because I look different?*

In my second year of medical school, I drive from Halifax to Oromocto as high as I've ever been, as high as I could be or dream of being, as angry and malevolent and joyful. Thinking fast, making impressionistic sense: as quickly as people leave one another, as they die or do harm, each thought somehow final on this five-hour drive. I walk the pathway to my parents' house, muttering mockingly of it as a "castle." I enter, slamming the heavy front door just as I remember my father slamming it so many times before. I keep my boots on, tracking dirt to the kitchen. *Shit under my feet,* I mutter. *Shit under my feet.* I pull out the cutlery drawer. Implements fall on the linoleum. I pick up a spoon not-spoon. I sit in my father's chair and place the spoon on the empty table. I tell the spoon that it is not a spoon. I bend it in half. I return the spoon back to the table, and leave it there. *Someone has been here*, it will say. *I am no longer a spoon*, it will say. I drive back to Halifax.

Ten years later, I eat supper with my parents in the dining room at 429 Gardiner. Cutlery now shakes in my father's hands; my mother retains her efficient, quick ease. Once again, I am wildly ill. Like the spoon, I have a purpose. Also like the spoon, I am in plain view. To begin, I look at my spoon and ask my mother calmly, *Is this a spoon?* She says, *What?* I ask my father the same question. He says, *Spoon, it's a spoon. Why? You want a fork?* I pick up the fork, imitating a famous dinner table Charlie Chaplin scene in which Chaplin makes cutlery dance. The forks, knives and spoons move about the table as if they are alive, with grace. I recall Chaplin's face: impassive, the look of a magician when asked to reveal his secrets. Fork asks Spoon, *Are you Spoon?* Spoon responds, *I am not Spoon. How dare you.* The nearby Knife consults Fork. *Is that guy Spoon?* Fork deliberates. *I am not sure. It appears as if they are a Spoon. But let us discover if they profess Spoon Philosophy.* Fork asks, *What is Spoon Philosophy?* I take Spoon from the table and hide it underneath. Knife leans conspiratorially towards Fork and whispers, *There is no Spoon.* Spoon taps underneath the table.

Other than the baseline affective state, in which I can be easily identified as possessing a crackling and morose energy overlaid on a facial blankness, my primary problem is interaction. Energy rises, boundless. The metaphor I use is *pushing*: I am pushed to interject in conversations, irresistibly steering conversation into insulting, antagonistic zones. I try to dominate the conversation to re-establish control over myself, but this only worsens what is already out of control.

To pass as normal, my strategy is to proceed through social space as if it were work. Work's rules provide comfort. There, I devised a mental thermometer to warn me, knowing I must take readings prospectively. Specific individuals tend to intensify negative feelings. I exert a strain not to care too much, not to talk too much. I try not to overinvest—and I do this every moment of the day when around people. Because I am pushed somehow to excess, I discipline myself to pull back. But if you were to look at me, you would think that I am inert, doing nothing.

In 2003, Christine Miserandino wrote "The Spoon Theory," an essay which metaphorized energy as "spoons." Her theory was developed when eating a meal, sitting across from a Normie who wanted to know what it was like to have a chronic invisible illness—a conversation so many of us are forced to have. The problem with such curiosity, forced as it often is to merely live in abstraction, is that people cannot transcend the gap of what they've never experienced. Metaphors—designed to carry knowledge across, etymologically speaking—are required. According to the legend, Miserandino develops the metaphor as follows: she starts by offering her curious friend a simple description of exhaustion and difficulty, which didn't help, especially since the person sitting across the table was a close friend and knew details of Miserandino's illness. To instill a more visceral understanding in the friend, Miserandino used the surroundings at hand. Spoons on the table became units holding energy, as if they contained sugar. According to the logic of spoons metaphor, the Normie is luxuriously outfitted with a full drawer, but the disabled person has a finite number, requiring them to husband their spoons.

I am not bad, though I was made to feel inadequate as a child—a pain that perpetuates itself and cannot be assuaged. My illness, less a diagnosis as pain but moreso an expression or echo of what was done, the aftereffects of an inception point, retains its moral dimension in the present but unfolds in a frame of relatively intensified invisibility. What previously was contested—what to call it back then? A major mental illness? Borderline personality disorder?—continues to invite contestation because the disturbance is less obvious now, less dramatic. My burden is like a mountain that grows larger, and yet no one can see the mountain. Such is the cost of relative wellness.

Because I lack a wheelchair, minor acquaintances ask me to perform my disability so that they "understand how I am disabled." For example: at a post-poetry reading party in October of 2019, following several exhausting hours of chatter with eager young businesspeople trying to pass themselves off as creatives, I defensively sit in a corner. I admire a bookshelf packed with American modernists. Some distance away, I overhear the homeowner, a scholar of twentieth-century American poetry, discoursing to the MFA-MA-MBA cohort in the kitchen in between shots of Jägermeister administered through a turkey baster. Fatally, an empty chair sits beside me. Though I have no idea why, a beautiful young woman—stylish white blouse, form-fitting pants, impeccable make-up—asks me: *Shane, why do you call yourself disabled?* The justification game is predicated on the lie of invisibility. I want to say, *If seeing is believing, people, then feast your eyes on this,* then strip naked and show them I am actually coloured green. Instead, I take Robert Lowell's *Life Studies* down from the middle shelf.

Lowell's breakthrough book is not overt proof of disability either, but it's the pure, beautiful feeling inside that I long to capture through my acts of writing. A restorative, spoon-filling feeling. I draw in a big breath and list "the things": clinical depression at the age of eight, in which I put a shotgun barrel in my mouth; a six-month continuous admission to a series of psychiatric hospitals in my twenties; the jump off the roof of a building; sensory overwhelmedness. The rendition concludes with, *And I suppose that, because I am no longer jumping off buildings, I am able.* What I often hear in response: *Nothing is perfect! Everyone gets low sometimes. I also had a hard time growing up. Oh, I find it hard to be in public too. I wish I could get away from it all every once in a while.* I replace *Life Studies* on the shelf and agree to help the woman with her short stories, the real point of the conversation. We both stand—time to get up and socialize. What she doesn't know is that I have to stand to get away from her, to end the conversation.

Thinking in magical terms, which I do, I now have in my house a drawer of many spoons. The supply is almost limitless. At night, when no one is looking, when everyone else is asleep, I open the drawer and run my hands over the spoons, recognizing slots for different sizes. Metal, plastic, sometimes a ting when curve hits against curve. The spoons are not wounds, not sad symbols from the past, but rather rehabilitated objects. Not points of contention, nor disputes about reality, control, and power, but instead little things no one needs to know about, hidden away, a contained theory of difference in inexhaustible supply.

I despise the word "invisible" because it is used divisively against people like myself. Not only does it pit the disabled against one another, creating hierarchies of physical and mental disability, but it also suggests that those with behavioural strangeness, non-neurotypical relations, passionate intensity, bizarre beliefs, and unusual sensory experiences are somehow invisible. But how is this so? The agoraphobic suffers indoors. Some call this invisibility. The homeless, who suffer very high rates of major mental illness, exist in plain sight. Yet somehow this is invisibility too? People who cannot, in the normate-conventional sense, be friends with other people due to non-reciprocal ways of relating to others are invisible? The people who cannot work at conventional 9-5 jobs because they are too impulsive or easily fatigued, you call this invisibility? Would it be simpler for you if we created a scarlet letter to mark difference so that it was easier to acknowledge? The scarlet letter already radiates out, even if it is not inscribed.

Every picture taken of me after age eight is an image I reject as false because the photographs are distorted by an energy I refuse to recognize as representative of myself. Instead, looking a little harder, I see what is always there under the smoked glass, a mind-body suffering that requires the word "invisibility" to invalidate it, to make it—and me—disappear. Relegation to margins takes visible work. "Invisible disability" is actually the product of *invisibilizing*. If I were so undetectably abnormal, why have I been pathologized throughout my life? Invisible disability is a contradiction that cannot be reconciled except by a mind subscribing to stigma.

On October 26, 2017, William Douglas Neilson died:

DAILYGLEANER.COM

LAWSON, BEULAH MAE

Beulah M. Lawson, formerly of Longs Creek, NB, wife of the late Charles A. Lawson passed away October 28, 2017 at Waukiehegan Manor, McAdam, NB, her home for the past three years. Beulah was born at Lake George, NB in 1925, a daughter of the late Lemuel and Frances (Courtney) MacLean.

She was a housewife but also employed at various local business. Beulah loved her cottage (little ... on Lake George and spent ... good times there with her family. ... was a member of the Ladies ... of McAdam ...

NEILSON, W. DOUGLAS

The passing of William Douglas "Doug" Neilson occurred on October 26, 2017, in Oromocto, NB. Born on January 9, 1942 in Sheffield, he was the son of the late Ralph and Sadie (Bridges) Neilson. He was the husband of the late Elizabeth (Foran) Neilson.

In Doug's early twenties, he joined the Royal Canadian Engineers and was stationed in Chilliwack, BC. In 1961 he was posted to Iserlohn, Germany ...

Within his obituary, I allude to a chasm of pain that made him restless, irritable, and possessed of a combustible insanity. In the name of truth, healing, and as a destigmatizing gesture for other ill persons in my home province who endure the same marginalization both he and I experienced, I wrote:

> Doug suffered from mental illness at points throughout his life. He experienced this illness during a period in [Canadian] history in which such illnesses are misunderstood and stigmatized. That prevented him from seeking and receiving the help that could have

> made his life more comfortable. His life was industrious, and Doug helped a great many people. But he also lost relationships and opportunities because of his illness, and his family hopes that anyone reading this obituary will be kind today to someone who is suffering.

My sister and I faced vigorous resistance to the publication of this document from other members of our family, who let us know that broadcasting the presence of "mental illness" would make their own lives more difficult—that *they* would endure stigma. Never mind that there is nothing to be ashamed of in the first place—how can anyone get better when such illnesses have people racing to re-stuff and then bolt the closets? To be neurodivergent does not entail a moral problem, but a lack of compassion shown the neurodivergent does. The reaction suggests what it would have been like for my father in rural New Brunswick in the 1940s and 50s.

You, too, would have run. Like he did. Like he made me do. In those long-ago worlds, affect hurt our bodies when it wished. What happened is always happening, ongoing; the emotion is ineradicable. All of this is visible. One just has to admit what one is seeing.

FACING QUESTIONS

Why does my brother have an easier time being around people?

> *Not "Why did people prefer your brother's company?" when growing up, but "Why wouldn't they have preferred him?"*

Why is everyone so serious around me?

> *Why don't you smile?*

What is serious?

> *Why is he so serious?*

Why am I alone?

> *Why are you so weird?*

Why do people call me "Rain Man"?

> *Are you listening?*

Why do I feel so in love with the world?

Why are you looking away?

Why do I not recognize my own face?

Someone less than human?

Why are photographs of me not me?

Aren't you what we say you are?

Why did my mother once ask me, "Maybe write out how you feel in a letter to your wife because, in writing, you can really express emotion"?

Is the explanation of any use other than understanding?

How much was never known because my body wouldn't disclose what I felt?

Is love even possible for people like you?

What is the right word to describe this kind of alone?

Can you blame other people for not knowing?

Why is poetry my preferred expression?

Does poetry even matter?

Are words all I have?

What use are words to the non-human?

Can a blank face contain poetry?

Isn't what's done, done?

Why do I feel different from your names?

Isn't what we told you all your life enough?

Why do I feel that it's important to distinguish *between* names?

Didn't our reactions to your difference offer enough names?

Is pain authenticating?

Are you saying you could learn a lot from us?

Do I owe it to the pain to name it correctly?

Can't you conceive of abuse as care?

Are you caring for yourselves as care?

What are your obligations to us?

Is it fair to raise children and feel immense love for them and to have a face like mine?

What are the evolutionary consequences to the human race in letting you share space with us?

Is it okay to just accept that my face will never change?

What do you think your face teaches your children?

Does it make sense that I can make it this long and have never been identified?

We didn't identify that you were different?

Is it that the one thing that I can do—express myself in written words—has allowed me to not be identified, my strength the reason I am in pain?

How long must we endure you?

If I had been diagnosed as a child would my life be different?

How is difference measured within that which is already different?

Would I have gotten as far?

Is "far" the right word?

Would I be happier?

How are we to blame?

Would my face be different now?

Isn't your face different now?

Would it be worse?

What could be worse than the non-human?

How fair is it for someone to be married to me and by extension, my face?

Why do you mourn what cannot be?

What is love with this face?

What technology exists to transform the non-human into human?

Is love words and actions only, or is it also how we are with one another?

What if the world is what we say it is, and you are what we say you are?

Is there an accommodation possible for inexpressivity?

How does one accommodate badness?

Not "Why me?" but "Why isn't the inherent goodness in me identifiable?"

Why shouldn't we discipline that which isn't like us?

Why do all the photos with my family, for whom I love, display *that* face, why is *it* there?

Why can't you be different than your difference?

Why am I different?

How do you feel?

Why do I feel different?

Do you feel anything?

Aren't my parents dead and the childhood bullies gone?

Can you feel?

BLURRING THE BORDERLINE

In the Nova Scotia Hospital, I am deemed

bad

even though I want to die, need to jump from a height, and, just a week later, do exactly that. The psychiatric staff consider me merely

parasuicidal

and record this in my chart. They also zestfully document my charged interactions with staff, my disdainful attitude and small resistances, concluding in each of their notes:

Cluster B.

This essay is not a critique of the professional opinions diagnosing a personality disorder, nor is it a celebration of the supposed disorder itself as it was/is applied to me, for I have a number of concerns about its name, history, and the reception of borderline diagnosis in medical culture, not to mention its applicability in my own case—a physician. Instead, this essay is an attempt to understand how we describe people who are suffering and how we might care for them better.

I have no memory of being on the ground. My wife later told me that circumstances would have been different, say, having hit the pavement a little to the left, where a short metal pole rose. But Janet pulled me back by my belt, and then my arms, altering my trajectory.

Do I sound like an embittered member of the psychiatric survivor movement? I hope not, because the overlap between borderline personality disorder (or BPD, existing in the proverbial Cluster B of the DSM-V, short form for *Diagnostic and Statistical Manual of Mental Disorders*, Fifth Edition) and bipolar disorder is significant, making accurate diagnosis difficult. Not only do 15 percent of borderline personality disorder patients get re-diagnosed later as having bipolar disorder, but symptoms can be remarkably similar. Think of the staff at the Nova Scotia Hospital encountering two fractionally different shades of red. Say, candy and rose. Some take one look at rose and, based on their own sweet tooth, they write down

> "candy"

in the chart. Then they see candy all day, every day, because they have decided:

> candy.

I try to throw myself through glass from the eighth floor of a different hospital.

A diagnostic criterion of bipolar disorder is experiencing periods of highs and lows that are outside the norms of variability and that last at least four days. The key to borderline personality disorder is also unstable mood, but on a much shorter timescale. Distinguishing nuance here is not always straightforward. I routinely encounter patients whom I suspect have borderline personality disorder, yet there is a tinge, a nag, that another underlying factor accounts for their presentation. I have also frequently seen patients with bipolar disorder who do less well on medication, whom I suspect (based on taking a careful history of their childhood) of having concurrent borderline personality disorder.

An orderly from the emergency department pulls me back from a concrete rampart where I would have fallen over forty feet.

The problem at bottom is twofold: first, the similarities and borderblurs between the two diagnoses; second, the fact that both diagnoses are more likely to occur if a child has a traumatic upbringing. Children who face adverse events develop a certain stance to the world, an oppositional and reactive one, often because they were never heard or soothed during their development. What Normies might call

drama

in a dysregulated acquaintance is not the acquaintance's perpetual dress rehearsal for life, a simulated scene the sufferer casts themselves (and everyone around them) in.

Drama

is, for some severely traumatized people, the only way to get through the day because the minor excitements of the present, no matter how self-created, pull the self away from the real pain of the past.

From 2004 to 2006, I unmake the makings of my Cluster B status, the judgement of self I agree is

bad—

because I *am*

bad,

I *am* repulsive, no one can love me – by meeting with Dr. J once a week for an hour or two, depending on his availability and the progress made in the moment. Rumpled, with tousled hair and a paunch, always wearing a golf shirt that could use one more button done up on the neck, the wise doctor provides simple medicine: he listens. I talk. Like most

bad

people, I have few others in my life who will listen; those who do quickly become overwhelmed. Negativity builds into a whirlwind, throwing everyone out of bounds. When I complete a sentence or two in his office in the Homewood, he laughs and says, *Really?* He means: *Why are you looking upon this so negatively? Why are you being so hard on yourself? Maybe what happened was just a step along the way, a lesson.* Of course, I resist, thinking: No way. I'm

bad.

You're wrong. What's true is that I am

bad.

To the layperson, the term "borderline" connotes a tendency to tip into psychosis, given the right conditions. Just push someone with BPD a bit too much, and they'll behave

crazy.

As it happens, this impression has both a substantiating historical basis as well as contemporary, real-world validation. In terms of history, the name was coined by Adolph Stern, an American psychoanalyst, who in 1938 built on Freud's conception of both "neurosis" and "psychosis" to synthesize a condition felt to be on the border between both. From the beginning, the diagnosis—different than the one that evolved to the present day—was felt to be rooted in a traumatic childhood. Stern hypothesized that, *It is not that these patients are exposed to specific experiences, sexual or otherwise, which are in themselves of a necessarily traumatic nature, but that their environment is...so traumatic that when they are exposed to such experiences they react to them as if they were traumatic.* In a very perceptive moment, Stern identified poor parental attachment and modelling in both mothers and fathers as a contributor to the development of BPD. The disorder is characterized by neglect, intermittent to absent attention, a severely critical and shaming parenting style, and serial rejections of the child. Today, a more complex formulation reigns: a genetic predisposition (in twin studies, BPD is highly heritable) in conjunction with a traumatic environment (including the aforementioned parenting deficiencies) is thought to create the condition. Since Stern, the diagnosis has undergone many re-conceptions. Initially, these revisions concerned the element of psychosis, and the thinking was that BPD was somehow a relative of schizophrenia. As more time passed, the diagnosis was refined in terms of behavioural description, and the core traits of what we know as the diagnosis today were described. Of particular interest is the fact that the most significant recent change to the diagnosis in the DSM-IV in 1994 involved the addition of the following criteria: the presence of *transient, stress-related paranoid ideation or severe dissociative symptoms.* In this way, history closes a loop and the border blurs once again between neurosis and psychosis. The preservation of "borderline" to the present day is an accident of history, a name echoing forward to the present even though it contains little (but not quite zero) descriptive usage. A better name is "emotion regulation disorder" because it accurately conveys the central symptom of the condition and is less pathologizing. Surely everyone can be a little emotional; what is unusual about going to the bar and getting hammered after being informed one's wife wants a divorce? That one's partner has just died in a car crash? Everyone seems susceptible under that kind of signalling rhetoric. Whereas people on the

borderline

are scary, just a hairsbreadth away from pulling a trigger.

Dr. J doesn't adopt a posture of certainty. Rather, he models openness. I start to question not only how I am

bad,

but if I am

bad

at all. If I utter such doubts aloud—like, *I wonder if I just did the best I could, under the circumstances?*—he smiles and says, *It's possible, isn't it?*

The story of Dr. Marsha Linehan, the creator of Dialectical Behaviour Therapy (DBT), is quite well known in psychiatric circles. The short version is: early in her life, Linehan received acute psychiatric care when in distress with BPD, including electroconvulsive therapy and carceral care. Her many negative encounters with physicians—invalidating, pathologizing, and harmful, though some were positive—spurred her to become a clinical psychologist to study the condition and develop a therapy for what was felt, at that point, to be untreatable.

Once, when an exchange is particularly charged, when his gently arch and skeptical attitude isn't enough to dampen my affect, Dr. J says, *Imagine you have a friend who is going through the same thing as you—exactly the same. He had the same childhood, he has the same mental illness, he's on the same kind of medication, he has a wife and a child, he's not working because he's so unwell. What would you say to him if he were in your situation?* Me: *I don't know. I never know what to do.* Dr. J: *Okay. Let's start at the beginning. What's his name?* Me: *I don't know. I don't have any good friends.* Dr. J: *Make one up. You choose.* Feeling disdainful of the idea of imagining a friend who never was, and who would never be, I say, *Ernesto!* Laughing, he says, *Okay. What do you say to Ernesto? He's really hurting.* Words come because for some reason I naturally care for this imaginary being, just like I care for all beings other than myself. Why should they suffer? Why should anyone suffer? Why must they be in pain? Surely something could help them, a word, an action? I say, *Ernesto, I know that it's hard now but it…will get better?* I speak uncertainly, speculatively. *That's not bad,* he says.

My most symptomatic BPD patients despise emergency departments. The reason is simple. Healthcare workers in such places are negatively predisposed to chronic mental problems that require intensive, long-term assistance. They tend to be disgusted by self-harm burns and lacerations. Many clinicians feel like the parasuicidal waste their time, or worse: one study found that 89 percent of psychiatric nurses described BPD patients as

manipulative.

Perhaps the most dear injury comes not with outrageous disdain or criticism, but with endemic invalidation: BPD patients do not feel they are being heard or believed when they seek care. Once again, re-enacting the processes of childhood, authority figures neglect, ignore, and minimize those who appear before them. History is always closing its own loop on the person with BPD, the past and present as one.

Each week, Dr. J parents me. How many

bad

people are lucky enough to get this kind of care? He assigns a video about a fat cartoon panda traveling down a river on a tube. Panda floats with the current, moving up and down the screen. Movement up means hyperarousal—bear's angry, irritated. Movement down is hypoarousal, meaning low mood, fatigue, isolation. In the sweet middle is the so-called Zone of Tolerance, where we can be happy, responding to the world on mutual terms. Where we're regulated, even happy. I want Panda to be happy, to stay in the safe middle, but he keeps bouncing up and down, stress shoving him up until he burns out and falls to the bottom, seesawing across the always-flowing river. Poor Panda. For some reason, Panda has a blue drop of moisture on his profile, either a tear or sweat, it's hard to tell. If only the word HAPPY, a bright yellow HAPPY, floated to him. If only the word were actually a cake and he could eat it and be happy. Dr. J. asks, *What did you learn from the video?* I tell him about the bright yellow word I imagined floating down the river, and he sighs. "If only it were that easy."

Essentialized, Dialectical Behaviour Therapy (DBT) is a kind of self-parenting program. Consider the signal moment Linehan personally identifies as the genesis of her idea for DBT: kneeling on a tussock at the Cenacle Center in Chicago where she found herself "looking up at the cross, and the whole place became gold—and suddenly I felt something coming toward me… It was this shimmering experience, and I just ran back to my room and said, 'I love myself.' It was the first time I remembered talking to myself in the first person. I felt transformed." Linehan didn't come to God here, she already had a deep spirituality that is often affirmed in *Building a Life Worth Living*, her memoir. Instead, the church enabled her to conceive of herself as worthy of love. At long last, Linehan realized she needed to approach herself with compassion. Linehan already believed God loved her. And she loved God. But she wasn't able to love herself. Now she was.

Similar kinds of childhoods create similar kinds of common futures. What we needed, way back when, was parenting. And truth be told, what we need now is the same.

Until relatively recently, Linehan attended psychiatric conferences as speaker and workshop leader, where—and I love this—she was querulous with psychiatrists.

Am I truly

bad?

Or do I get mixed manic, the kind of high that wants to destroy everything in its path: relationships, career, finances—all love. I try to respond to myself like a parent would, since I have to parent myself now—in a way, I've always had to. I say, *Things were really difficult, but you did a lot of work and now you know to be kind to yourself. What would you say to Ernesto?* I respond to myself, *There there, Ernesto. Everything will be okay.*

The risk of suicidality in borderline personality disorder is 43.7 percent. The risk of suicidality in bipolar disorder is 30 percent. Suicidality risk in comorbid borderline personality disorder and bipolar disorder is 44.7 percent. Seventy-five percent of BPD patients attempt suicide in their life. Ten percent actually complete the act. Almost 20 percent of bipolar patients die by suicide.

Everything will be okay.

Appearing regularly in the nursing notes from the Nova Scotia Hospital is an expressed worry about the possibility of violence. Caregivers speculate whether I have ever struck my wife or daughter even though I express no willingness to harm anyone. I am merely sad, but the esteemed caregivers feel a need to confirm that I am not harming my family. A record of an interview with my wife verifies that I am not harming her.

1:1 with writer and indicated his anger and frustration at the meeting this morning, feels that his caregivers do not understand his marriage—was unhappy at how his interviewers cut him off—analyzing each sentence—Shane indicated that his manner of speech—normally—is circumvoluting—cutting him off after initial statement meant that he was not able to fully express himself—Suggested that he needed to be more direct and Shane was unhappy with this—indicated that he had been this way all his life and wasn't about to change particularly about the "fucking" eye contact—requests for eye contact really, really annoyed him. Like his manner of speech, Shane feels that he has always declined to meet anyone's eyes "except for my patients" and while it might seem aloof to others—this was his normal demeanour.

Reviewing the log's multiple iterations of

Cluster B

years later, I begin to feel as if the words are somehow righteous, a mark of real distinction, representing all of one man's understandable reaction to carceral care, disinterested licensed practical nurses, observed medication compliance, and lack of grounds privileges that, of course, was alchemized into blame. I invert the phrase to signify criticism of the institution, not the patient:

badness.

Anything I would say in protest of the judgement of my character got recorded in the chart, accompanied by a description of tone

(angry)

(aggressive).

Daily, this: everything will be okay. Don't think everything will be

bad,

that you are

bad.

You're doing your best, and when you aren't, you'll know. At those times, you choose not to try, and you rarely so choose. Instead, you almost always tell yourself you aren't good, that you are

bad.

But that's not true. The tragedy is that you are good, but you cannot see the fact, you cannot let yourself see it. Long ago, the people who should have cared for you constructed a version of you—let's call him bad—

that organized the rest of your life. What can you be without that false identity? Perhaps as you always were, someone who just needed a little soothing, way back when. Soothe yourself now. Tell yourself that everything will be okay.

TWO-HIT HYPOTHESIS

After failing to impress in interviews for medical school across Canada, I am asked to re-interview at Dalhousie University because, I am told, my first attempt *was completely discordant from the letters about your character.* The people who wrote my reference letters know me well. My next-door neighbour, Ed. My boss at the Sir Hugh John Fleming Forestry Centre, Taumey. My mentor in biochemistry, Margarida. Dalhousie says: *Your marks put you close to the top of the applicant pool, but your interview rated poorly. The interviewers thought you were aloof, too distant to practice medicine. Lacking empathy.* In return, I tell them that during my first interview, one of the epidemiologists took a consult. For about ten minutes, he talked on the phone about chlamydia as the other epidemiologist whispered his questions, encouraging me to answer, but pushing his hand down when I spoke, as if I should whisper too. When they asked me at the end of the interview if I had any questions for them, I asked for their opinion about the effect of recently deployed Video Lottery Terminals in Nova Scotia. My question was prompted by genuine curiosity, and also by the view of the Halifax Casino, perhaps half a kilometre away. *Why would you want to know about that?* they asked.

Well, I said, a lot of people in New Brunswick are getting addicted. Go into any bar there, really, and watch the poor souls drop loonies in slots for hours at a time. *We really couldn't say*, they replied. Their research was in chlamydia only, it seems. I wondered what kind of doctor isn't curious about their own field and how it applies in their own backyard, within their literal view? Me, I take pride in where I come from, and I know health is more than disease. Two weeks after my re-interview, I received an offer from Dalhousie. A two-hit hypothesis applies to my success: if the procedural botch hadn't have happened, and if I didn't form strong relationships with a handful of individual people over long periods of time, then I wouldn't have become a doctor, easily weeded out of an admissions regime hostile to the non-neurotypical. A savvier student would have pivoted quickly to ask a question about chlamydia, would have been able to mask their irritation at being dismissed, at being disrespected. A cunning student would have known that the objective was to get the interviewers to like you. Tell me everything about chlamydia, I love it, o chlamydia guru. Tell me about the perils of screening and not following up for test of cure.

*

That summer, I move from Oromocto to Halifax for medical school. Four months pass before I talk to another student outside of class. I walk the twenty-five minutes from my two-storey post-WWI brick home on Summer Street to the Tupper Building and back, neither happy nor sad, neither excited nor fearful. I lack a vocabulary to even conceive of autism. I just want to learn. I believe that learning is all that's required of me, which is very wrong. What is required I cannot give, normativity not being there to offer. How to screen for what is there and what isn't? I am the false positive, the student that shouldn't be.

*

Medical school requires learning in groups, *teams*, but I find conversations involving more than one person difficult. I am disoriented by certain kinds of artificial lighting; some high-register sounds completely overwhelm me; vocal tone is tricky to interpret. Worst of all for social reciprocity, I can talk for far too long, in great paragraphical gusts. In my third month of school, I am taken aside by a preceptor. *There's something wrong with you*, he says. *And I talked with someone else who has observed you. They think the same.* I am being screened out. The implicit message academic medicine sends me about my general badness, my unsuitability, is: "You're autistic, we hate that." But because medicine at that time—and up to the present—prefers not to diagnose non-neurotypicality, avoiding naming the unholy state altogether, I was left to my own devices to reason that the preceptor meant "difficult" and "unprofessional." Autism is a diagnosis that medicine dares not name but instead misidentifies because it doesn't understand. The establishment prefers the norm because of medicine's own epistemology. Medicine diagnoses things it disdains as *bad*, and in the process misdiagnoses that which it should cherish and care for. There's no diagnostic process for care, though, just impressions and registrations of it.

*

In my second year as a medical student, I walk to a meeting with the undergraduate dean and the rest of the promotions committee. Along the way, I consider throwing myself under the wheels of a passing car on Robie Street. And then the next car. The next. Next. A luxurious line of cars. I had just roused myself from bed after two weeks in which I rose only to use the bathroom or to drink. I lack a vocabulary to explain that I am both bipolar and autistic, meaning that I experience extremes of emotion and yet cannot identify or describe highs and lows. The medical term for such a state is alexithymia, defined in the *OED* as "The inability to recognize one's own emotions and to express them, esp. in words." Curiously, the word was invented in 1974, one year before I was born, as if the entry were followed by a blank that would later be filled in with my name.

Alexithyma ______.

Even if I had a vocabulary back then, I wouldn't have confessed the fact. Medicine's culture of toxic professionalism means that I may be admitting to some administrator's eventual designation of permanent unsuitability to the role. *He's bad*, they might say, shrugging their shoulders. *He says so himself. This is a good decision. Good for patients.*

*

I express life in the form of equations. Normative people use narrative as their tool to understand the world; I use equal signs. For example, the Simple Balancing Equation That Explains All Things is:

> this (bad) crazy person does (crazy) bad things = they are a crazy bad person = they are (crazy) bad in character = their actions are (crazy) bad

*

Because I miss a deadline near the end of medical school due to an unconfessed passion to die, the powers that be command me to complete a remedial project on professionalism. I must write a paper commenting on the evidence attesting to the persistence of unprofessional behaviours in medical students into their practising careers—the equivalent of Bart Simpson transcribing 100,000 lines of *I must not grow up to be a bad doctor.* Yet I cannot help but question the frame as I take my punishment:

I must not grow up to be a bad doctor.
I must not grow up to be a bad doctor.

What is a bad doctor?

I must not grow up to be a bad doctor.
I must not grow up to be a bad doctor.

What does it mean to be "bad" in medicine?

I must not grow up to be a bad doctor.
I must not grow up to be a bad doctor.

What is meant by "bad," and for whom?

I must not grow up to be a bad doctor.
I must not grow up to be a bad doctor.

I am not writing my required lines. I will not complete the task.

I must not grow up to be a bad doctor.
I must not grow up to be a bad doctor.

I pass, but a month later than the rest of my colleagues, receiving my diploma in the mail. For the next two years of my subsequent family medicine residency, I remain that exact month behind everyone else. I must explain the reason for my latency when arriving on every new rotation, unprofessionalism a scarlet "U" on my forehead—my blank, expressionless forehead.

*

While living in the [Undisclosed Hospital Name] for the fifth and penultimate month of my second admission, the latter occurring during an additional year training as an R3 in the Emergency department, a Great West Life agent expects me to call and provide information about my clinical case and background to substantiate a disability claim. I had jumped off a building when in a mixed manic state. Prior to that, I thought my wife was trying to kill me, that she would stab me in the chest when I was asleep. I have issues with simple coherence, yet I must tell him these things. I slam the phone down on him. Alexithymia, rage, action speaks louder. The claim is approved. Finally, I am a true positive.

*

In the years since graduating from Dalhousie, I return to Halifax many times. I cannot look at the many hospitals—VG, New Halifax Infirmary, Abbie Lane, Camp Hill, Dartmouth General—when I drive past them. They are the sites of my own despising, where I learned to believe in my own unsuitability. The aversion to looking at them remains strong to this day, as if I resist pushing my eyes into a buzzsaw.

*

From 2005 to 2011, I work as a family physician in a rural Ontario community. Perhaps twice a year, I have difficulty concentrating and my mood dips such that I feel I would not be doing a service to my patients by pretending to be well. I miss a few days or at most a week of work and return ready, somewhat replenished. After one missed October week, an elderly patient returns for a follow-up after being seen by my locum a few days before. He seems angry, even though his impressive right foot infection noted in the chart five days ago has improved to today's dim suppurative glow. As I inspect the wound, he growls, *So where did you go last week? I asked the replacement doc if you were okay. I mean, you're not supposed to worry about doctors. But I guess I have to. Is there something wrong with you?* Any interruption of service results in patients wanting to know why, creating amongst providers a culture of destructive health, of supposed iron constitutions and camouflaged illnesses. I figure I am getting the usual guff, i.e. "Where were you in my hour of need, and why won't you be there forevermore?" But something about this question comes at me the wrong way. *What did he tell you?* I ask. *He's hiding, that doctor said. He's hiding. So, were you? Hiding?*

*

I submit a paper on autism in physicians to a medical journal and receive the following feedback: *I prefer to think about people with various abilities. You have a freakish ability with language. I have a peculiar ability in music, but for various reasons I don't make a living at playing the piano. If we were living in the world of Thomas More's* Utopia *(some might say dystopia), we would be diagnosed with these abilities and supported solely on this basis. Funny how our society has evolved a strong system for reinforcing and policing disabilities, but not so much for abilities.* Diagnosed on abilities? That is a dystopia, the current one.

*

Some nights I suffer a nightmare in which I move provinces due to my wife's occupation and must fill out a new medical college's registration application concerning fitness to practice, rather than just completing the yearly update from the current College of Physicians and Surgeons of Ontario. How does a chronic, relapsing (but also daily) illness please the college? Tick an ill-fitting box to please the college. How does a developmental disorder please the college? Tick a grotesque box to please the college. The purpose of a college's screening questionnaire is, to one way of thinking, to "protect" Canadians from unscrupulous, incompetent, and/or ill physicians. From badness. For people like me, the purpose is to screen out alterity, to cure a mistake made long ago. When I wake, I'm left wondering how I might plead my case to the college's registration committee; how I might recruit its Physician Health Program to be an advocate, knowing the chances are poor, for neither have the most rudimentary knowledge of disability studies. Can a balance be struck between the college's duty to protect the public on the one hand and the needs of physicians who have chronic mental illnesses and/or non-neurotypicality on the other? Is there a way to trust the college to sort through what it *calls* impairment, and what its subjects would *experience* as impairment? How can the public's expectation of professionalism from its practitioners be reconciled with stigma? How might we reasonably accommodate ill and non-normative practitioners? What kind of professional class and culture are we creating if lived experience is stigmatized and actively punished?

*

Three years after my patient accuses me of hiding, while attending a recovery maintenance meeting, I encounter my former locum in the mental hospital, yellow bracelet on his left arm. He was admitted three days before.

*

In 2015, I publish *On Shaving Off His Face,* a book of poetry with The Porcupine's Quill that considers the iconography of the face in mental illness. One of the poems, "Three Essays Facing One Another," enters the minds of Adam Lanza, Jared Loughner, and Seung-Hui Cho, three American mass shooters with mental illness. Of mental illness. Badness. In a fancy Toronto academic publication, a reviewer writes: *In his practice as in his book he deals in mental illness—assumedly he tries to alleviate it—and this raises questions of professional ethics when the professional is also a poet. What if someone reads* On Shaving Off His Face—*doubtless his patients would be curious to read their doctor's book, but let's say this someone is anyone—and, as it so obviously intends, it strikes the reader with the full force of its intelligent and suppressed fury, which exacerbates the reader's mental illness? That's the kind of conflict of interest that needn't be resolved to be productive, as long as you're not on the wrong side of the trigger.* The message is clear: I am discouraged from speaking. Write about mental illness? Well, it will spread! It will incite homicide! You must be a perfect, pristine model to your patients. You may not be ill, and if you are, you must never speak its name. To engage with your illness aesthetically, honestly, challengingly, is to encourage the worst, most catastrophic outcomes to occur. *Be silent* is a message I have received over and over in my life, from within medicine but also, obviously, without. The reviewer insinuates that for me as a physician, as opposed to a host of other artists, it is unethical to make art about suffering. What would my college think of this review if it were included to substantiate a complaint?

*

For most of my life, I avoided academic medicine, afraid I would be caught out as odd, strange, weird, unprofessional, screened into the saw. Yet 2016 is the start of something new, something *good.* I now know a clinching name for my difference, acquiring "autism" along the way as a gleaming key to all understanding, a Rosetta Stone for all baffling past experiences. Medical norms have labelled me "unprofessional," when what I am is "non-normative." When the norm says my name, it means *bad.* Bipolar disorder never provided a synthesis for how I was perceived in medicine or in life. The addition of autism came less as label and more as means to offer self-compassion. *I am not bad*, I could tell myself. I am different in a way medicine cannot tolerate. I am good for patients who are like me. I am less likely to dismiss them. I have more patience. To stop hearing the sound of the buzzsaw, I start participating in hospitals and school spaces to make it okay to be different. I begin to care for myself analogously, as if I am able to enter a time machine simply by walking around a medical school and teaching there, soothing my earlier self by doing so, the student-me continuous with practising-me in the present.

*

Back in Halifax, at a medical school reunion, my specialist friend's fancy sports car takes turns like it's on rails. As we cross the Macdonald Bridge, he tells me a story. I'm not sure why he's telling it. Until I am. *There was this young woman who was dying. She had a head injury and was in shock. Everybody in the unit knew there was no coming back. The bleed was massive. Three separate skull fractures. But she was still alive. And we didn't want to run a code on her. Anyways, we get her from emerg, and we're looking for next of kin. In comes her parents—and they're both drunk. As in, reeling drunk. I have to have a conversation with them even though they're out of it. I have to talk to them about code status even though they stink of alcohol. And they're causing problems for the nurses whenever they visit their daughter, and the nurses complain to me about it. In the end, I had to take them into the family room and just tell them to get it together, that their daughter was dying and the least they could do for her was to not come into the hospital drunk.* Nausea rose in my body as we took more turns, then falling as we made straightaways. I let the stigmatizing story pass without comment. First, I wondered: is this what he thinks of me—someone who couldn't and can't "get it together?" A beat later, I realized the true moral: the suffering persons in the story are not the care team.

*

Now that I have passed into the medical education stronghold, I am privy to problematic conversations about disabled students. Overheard on Zoom in 2021: a group of physicians discuss professionalism in medical students with multiple psychiatric and developmental comorbidities. *It's unfair to them, to the students. To have them in an impossible situation where they cannot succeed. How can they relate to patients? How can they inspire confidence? It's better to explain to them that they may be better off not being doctors.* In the chat, I write: "I am awed by your profound virtue and noblesse oblige. Thank you for caring so much for the ill and autistic students among us. After all, the mentally ill and autistic patients we practising physicians care for should know that we truly cherish medical students like them by acts like banishment." As I wrote, I heard this voice in my ear: *We, the good, do this for you, the bad.* I suffered. My family suffered. But I knew I wasn't bad. My patients and those who trusted me knew I wasn't bad. And now the next generations of doctors are starting to know it, too. In 2023, a group of McMaster students write me about an article they plan to publish in *CMAJ* about neuroatypicality and the disciplinary practices of medicine. *We were encouraged to approach you as a faculty contact,* they write. *You have lived experience that might speak to our lived experience. There aren't any other faculty members that self-identify.* The irony: my professional identity somehow consolidates *as* professional, but on disability's terms.

*

A year later, I am interviewed by the editor-in-chief of the *Canadian Medical Association Journal* on ableism in the medical profession, the occasion being an article I just published in the journal about all the times I had been stigmatized in professional spaces for being unwell and non-neurotypical. During the meeting, I disclosed to the editor, who also identifies as non-neurotypical, that I hoped the piece would contribute to the slow improvement happening in the profession concerning ableism. The interview doesn't touch anecdotes I can't tell, stories I can't tell you either.

*

A day later, a young resident called me, given my number by a colleague who wanted to connect a struggling learner with someone who had lived experience. The resident wanted to do an additional year of training in the emergency department, but worried about what would happen based on the evaporation of a sleep schedule. I told them that I, too, went through the additional year of residency, but had to give up the prospect of such a career based on sleep disruption. I added, "I just couldn't imagine a future when a group of colleagues were cool when I didn't do night shifts like them. And I don't think that's changed."

*

At a presentation during a continuing medical education event, the speaker—a formidable intensivist with decades of experience—provides a mini-history of relevant (and, naturally, recent) milestones in the history of accommodations in medicine. Like Dr. Jessica Dunkley, the Métis dermatologist who took the University of British Columbia to the BC Human Rights Tribunal to be accommodated in her residency program as a deaf learner. Like Dr. Chad Ruffin, the deaf American ENT surgeon. "If my kids had to get cochlear implants," the intensivist said, "I would want them to see that surgeon." This message—that inclusion brings with it value to patients—was doubled with a practical, institutional message against legal exposure. The intensivist relayed the long, court-proven truth that if a valid accommodation is slow-walked or denied, the academic institution is vulnerable.

The intensivist neutrally relays further material, her tone likely chosen from long experience. Observations like the profession's longstanding preference for accepting "physical" accommodations (to a limit), rather than "mental" accommodation; the profession's "curiosity" around making diagnoses that would best explain a student's accommodations. "It's the doctor in us," she laughs, as if we can't help but use our knowledge to solve a puzzle.

Thus far, I was satisfied with academic medicine in its continuing medical education incarnation. The institution's representative was calm, effective, self-identified as invisibly disabled, and knew the history of struggle for disabled people. Then, she presented a case to this group of academic physicians responsible for the learning of medical students and residents. From the slides:

> Student 1 is a Postgraduate Year Two (PGY2) who has had academic struggles in your program since Postgraduate Year One (PGY1) and has undergone remediation twice. She has recently provided medical documentation for the first time which indicates functional impairments including: poor concentration, difficulty with organization, planning, and time management skills, and also difficulty with sleeping/waking.
>
> The following accommodations have been approved on a temporary basis for the next three months: increased time per patient (double the amount usually given to a PGY2), reduced number of patients per half day clinic (half the amount a PGY2 would normally see), and templates to assist with documentation as well as double the time for documentation.

> You have received this information, as Student 1's clinical supervisor in Family Medicine for the next two weeks. 1. What will you do on the first day of the rotation? 2. Who else on your team needs to know this information? 3. What if you hear other students "grumbling" about the fact that Student 1 has more time in clinic to see patients and complete documentation by the end of the day?

After reading the case and questions, the intensivist asks, "So, what would you do?" and for perhaps five seconds, there is silence. Then, Really Guy raises his hand to save us all. Really Guy says, "Really… ?" His is a rhetorical question, as if there were a fill-in-the-blank answer afterward we should all mentally complete.

> Like this: *Really* ________?

> A few beats later, he adds: "I mean, I don't want to be evil, but… *really* ________?

For him, the answer is self-evident, a fill-in-the-blank that biomedical training already presupposes, that creates the conditions such that it need never be said aloud, that makes it impossible for a student to thrive, that makes that blank an absence, a vacuum pulling a student into space, far away from patients.

The intensivist is unsure if she is to just respond to what seems like a blanket rejection of the premise of accommodation, or of the idea of illness entirely, or the lack of a death machine, or what. He appears early-forties, is sitting next to three much younger female professionals in the room, all of them pretty and fit. The intensivist starts to speak, but is overridden. "I mean, again, I don't want to be evil. Maybe it's just that I'm an old guy…" Also like this:

> I mean, again, I don't want to be evil. Maybe it's just that I'm an old guy… ________.

Compared to the doctors in his row, he was indeed old. It didn't stop him from sitting next to them. "I guess I mean to say, *Really* _______? How can such a student function in *my* busy emergency department ________? How can they contribute ________? If I were asked to take on such a student, I would turn them down."

My chest begins to hurt. A strong, spreading pressure, a clamp. "Thank you for being so honest," the intensivist says. "If you're saying it out loud, then I guarantee many other people in the room are thinking it." She looks as I'd expect her to look—ready. She's heard this before, confronted it before. Many, many times before.

The chest pain intensifies, I find it harder to draw breath. I also find it harder to reason, for the same force crushing my torso is squeezing the thoughts out of my mind: *Really, because you are temporarily able _____. What if you find yourself in the same circumstances, soon _____? What if you cheat on your partner with the buxom blonde next to you in the clean utility room, and you get divorced, and you lose access to your children, and you drink too much, and you get depressed ______? Should we never let you work again, since you'd be a burden to your colleagues ______?* The chest pain adopts a throbbing quality. A dull throb. I begin to fear that other people around me can hear a wheeze. *Really, because how are we to try to live up to the supposed compassionate ideals of our profession, if we cannot be compassionate to one another _____?*

Isn't compassion false unless it is held also for ourselves _____? If we do not practice it on ourselves, on one another _____?

I am, now, seeing stars; the urge to speak is rising in my body, an irresistible pressure. But behind me, I know, is a very inclusive and compassionate dean; also, a workplace colleague that fights every day to accommodate ill medical students; finally, our continuing medical education coordinator who, almost certainly, doesn't need my disruption. Most of all, I know this isn't safe—if I were to speak, a lifetime of abuse would come like a fist out of my mouth. I can feel it right now, coiling in my chest. *Really, because patients themselves sense our ableist attitudes baked into our ontology ________. We treat one another terribly, demanding only a perfect competence, perfect health, so as to process ill people efficiently ________. But what is our process _______? Our process is to show disabled people, a demographic the least satisfied with the socialized system based on having the greatest exposure to it, that we do not tolerate disability amongst ourselves ________. They will never trust us until we trust them to be us _______. Really _______. Wait a minute ________. You have this backward ________. You should never have the opportunity to turn down students ________. Thank your for telling on yourself, really _______. You should not have the privilege of teaching at all _______. Really _______.*

All that's keeping me from hyperventilating, falling over, and then being acknowledged, and then perhaps having to unleash an embarrassing torrent of righteous disdain at Really Guy, or worse, confirming Really Guy's attitude, is the word "really" itself. My hand, subtly on my chest in the way Dr. J has encouraged, splayed, feeling a slight warmth, a more noticeable rise and fall, is there to reinforce the message. *Really. Really. Really. Really. Really.* I think of some of the ill physicians I personally know whom have returned to practice. Hundreds. How desperate they were to show they remained competent, how dedicated, how badly they wanted to be recognized as normal, as good. How they bucked their restrictions on return to work, how they resented their accommodations, how lucky they, we, and patients were to have a professional overseer insisting that boundaries were kept. These physicians, to a one, did not want to be seen as weak, which was part of why they got so sick to begin with. They also didn't want lower expectations. They had internalized those expectations, making them like a solemn promise they had taken with life itself. They wanted to deliver good care. They just needed accommodation to do so. But for you, Really Guy, and all the others like you, accommodations are weakness, unsuitability, a burden.

My phone says twenty minutes have passed. Somehow, there is a new presenter at the front of the room, a young Asian man. The slide says *Mentoring in Medicine* and there is a picture of a gym locker, football helmet inside. "Describe a moment when a coach made a significant difference in your life," he asks the audience. No one answers, so I put up my hand and say, in a slow, deliberate voice:

> I was nine years old. Little League, in Oromocto, New Brunswick. I would go to the plate and each time, I struck out. I never swung the bat. This went on for two months, and other players would laugh; it was so bad, other parents would groan on the stands, or even encourage the pitcher to just lob it quickly so they could get me out. The thing was, I was scared to swing the bat. I couldn't do it. One day, a parent came out of the stands. He stood next to me and said, "I'm going to help you swing the

> bat." He said it matter-of-factly, kindly. He put his hands over mine, and when the pitch came, we connected early on the ball, knocking it just right of the third base line, past the baseman and into the outfield. I always swung the bat after that, and I became a fairly okay baseball player. Not great, but good enough to play.

In this moment, I somehow fused timelines according to trauma chronology:

> Jumping ahead to medicine, I suppose you could say I didn't belong, that I wasn't like the other kids, that I should just go away. But just like that father who came down and helped me swing the bat, I found the people in medicine who helped me too.

*

I tell Dr. J about Really Guy. Dr. J really likes the nickname. He laughs. I really am a card. Outside the bay window of his basement, a verdant Elora backyard conjures the impossibility of an idyll. The fishtank behind and to the right of Dr. J's head lacks its usual soothing quality, for it has interlopers—graceful, wispy angelfish have been added, their black feelers brushing against the neon mutants. *I picked angelfish because they're a species that can swim backward*, he says. Is this a subtle therapeutic message? After I vent about Really Guy for a few minutes more, he asks, *What's behind your reaction to Really Guy?* I say, *I've been working against a guy like that all my life, in medicine and outside. People like that believe I don't belong anywhere they are.* I feel a need to punctuate the statement: *FUCK Really Guy*, I say. Dr. J provides me the answer to my question earlier—yes, his choice of fish was meaningful. *You know, your reaction to Really Guy is probably some kind of rejection of yourself, that you suspect that Really Guy might be correct on some level. Maybe you need to consider how your experiences are valuable, how they are helping the world right now*. And in me, my own Really Guy takes my neck. And squeezes.

CHIRON THE WOUNDED HEALER

My wound clamours to tell you something:

> Shane wishes to be rid of rivenness. Like most Bearers who have not learned enough, he wants me to go away completely, totally. But just as Bearers cannot ever be a totality of shame, Shane cannot dispense of that which has been done. He can only acknowledge and incorporate. Substances, sex, countless distractions, yet Shane can never be free from that which he is: broken. He cannot be healed. He might live with me productively; he might not. Bearers are free to use us (me). They are free to let us (me) sink below the skin, but we (I) control the world there. He must listen to the hum.

*

The modern origin of the wounded healer archetype is popularly attributed to Carl Jung, who wrote in *Fundamental Problems in Psychotherapy* that "the physician who heals wounds is himself the bearer of a wound, a classic example being Chiron." Yet Jung is not the Chiron's original latter-day herald. In his book, Jung thanks Prof. C. Kerényi who "kindly lent me the MS. of his work" on "the primordial physician as the 'wounded healer,'" mentioning "Chiron, Machaon, etc." Jung refers here to a text eventually published in English translation as *Asklepios; archetypal image of the physician's existence*. I own a copy as shield, bearing it as such on difficult days, holding it up to the sun from my back window. At other times, I rub the cover as a means to honour wounds. *There, there. Everything will be okay.* The thick, rough bookcloth siphons thought. (Sometimes wounds prefer silence.)

*

The Precepts of Chiron is a fragmentary text attributed to Hesiod, who wrote the didactic work in the voice of Chiron; Achilles is the pupil addressed. The full and true *Precepts* has been lost, a few fragments preserved only in quotation by other authors. In this way, the text itself is modelled as a wound. The wound disappears, in one sense, through healing, yet it can never disappear, always in conversation with others.

*

My wound dislikes speech. The most it has to offer was given at the outset of this essay. Generally, it either listens or waxes and wanes in my body depending on how much I myself listen. A strangulating feeling in my throat. Coursing lactic acid rivulets in my legs. In great distress—when an image of a water tower or a bridge railing insert in my mind—the wound will play a film for me. I will see, and then somehow feel, the caress of willow branches on my forehead and back. My wife's hands, tracing circles on my temples. Fingertips against Kerényi's shield, the treatise on Chiron. All instant, dissociative portals that pull into a holding place.

*

After learning of the influence of Kerényi on Jung, I naturally wanted to learn more about Kerényi the man, and information about him has proven elusive. After an extensive search, reading book after book by Kerényi who preferred to not self-disclose, I discovered *Essays in Memory of Karl Kerényi* as edited by Edgar C. Polomé, existing only as an issue of the *Journal of Indo-European Studies*. This issue is incredibly rare and as fate would have it, I believe I possess Polomé's own copy. Pristine and without marginalia or markings, the front page features a taped-on insert made of the same gold cover material bearing Polomé's stamp, placed exactly where an author would strike their typeset name and inscribe their signature. Here is the stamp text exactly as it appears orthographically, lacking as it does the proper accent for Polomé's name (as it is a stamp made in North America, I presume) and wounding the terminus of the second line due to an errant hand-cut with scissors:

PROFESSOR EDGAR C. POLOME
DEPARTMENT OF ORIENTAL LANGUAG
UNIVERSITY OF TEXAS AT AUSTIN
AUSTIN, TEXAS 78712
(USA)

I prefer to think the error as intentional, not an error at all. A deliberate wounding of language.

*

In *Fundamental Problems in Psychotherapy*, Jung elaborates on the process of wounded healing as a participatory act in which the physician does as much work as the patient. He begins by offering what could be a gloss on Christ's analogy in Luke 4:23, "Physician, heal thyself!" For Jung, the psychotherapist must first identify wounds and attend to them in an alert, active way: "a good half of every treatment that probes at all deeply consists in the doctor examining himself, for only what he can put right in himself can he hope to put right in the patient." A doctor's own psychological conflicts can react either with or against a patient's own. *Against*, if the doctor hasn't processed them and they operate completely unconsciously; *with*, if the doctor has meaningfully addressed and maintained them. For the dialectical process to work, the doctor's own history, their being, something almost undiscussed, something submerged (Chiron secretly acting under the skin as the god of wounds) activates the patient's own capacity for healing, a healer that lives in their wounds. The physician's experienced wound shows the naïve wound how to heal, yet there is less of a hierarchy as one might think. The wounds do not insist on rank, for the physician's wound is *tended to* in the act of *tending for*. A harmonizing of wounds.

*

The first fragment of *Precepts* was copied by a scholiast in the margin of a text by Pindar: *And now, pray, mark all these things well in a wise heart. First, whenever you come to your house, offer good sacrifices to the eternal gods.* Though the meaning of the statement is obvious—be in alignment with the world, humble and awestruck—it is the detail of persistence as anonymous marginalia that I love. A priest, pastor, or political demagogue might command, *Be kind*, and I would ignore them. Why listen? They are common. Paid. They hide wounds, would never admit to being partial, lacking, damaged, broken. But if I encountered two words, *Be kind,* scrawled in a cursive mashed near the center margin of a secondhand book—a sci-fi pulp novel from the 1930s, or my mother's Danielle Steele hardcovers in the basement—I would feel indeed as if I were being advised by the gods. By Chiron.

*

In my therapist's room, I learn the reason for the aquarium changeover from neon aliens to wispy anglerfish. The mutation that authored their beautiful flare shortened their life. How may myths tell this tale? Achilles, who could have lived a long, uneventful life. Phaethon, mortal son of Helios, and his chariot across the sky. Icarus in the sky with diamonds. *Ignus fatuus*, the "foolish flame," friar's lantern, hinkypunk, jack o'lantern, *feu follet*, *irrlicht*, or as I knew it as a child, will-o'-the-wisp over the Portobello Creek. Willows. Anglerfish wisps. Atmospheric ghost light in the holding place.

*

The wounded healer archetype reconstituted itself over time. Examples can be found in Norse tales, Arthurian legends, and of course Christianity itself, where Jesus is the "Great Physician" in Mark 2:17. Of course, the archetype is not purely a Western one. How could it be? The dog-goddess Gula/Labartu of Babylonian mythology. Kali, Hindu goddess. The ritual of *Thwasa* by the Xhosa, which induces illness states to become *igquri*—a healer. To exploit those traditions as a mythology colonist, interpreting traditions I have not lived, would wound the archetype I explore. I would defeat myself in the exploitation, I would create a wound. So I write instead of a centaur imagined by the Ancient Greeks, their culture informing the language used by contemporary Western physicians. And because I cannot escape the pull of my own Catholic childhood, the weight of the crucifix currently pulling on my neck, I write of that system too as absorbed in the family pew at St. Vincent de Paul in Oromocto, New Brunswick—right side, ten down.

*

Chiron's legend persisted because poets kept his being alive. Not his legend, not his story, but his *being*—Homer, Pindar, Hesiod, and many others. Chiron is not the first "wounded healer" in actuality. Poets are our wounded healers. They carried the myths for us to heal; they write cultural diagnostics for us now; their art is itself a means of possible healing. In their poems, they harmonize wounds.

*

In the introduction to *Essays in Memory of Karl Kerényi,* Polomé mentions that Kerényi was asked to join the board of the *Journal of Indo-European Studies* at its inception, and he agreed "graciously" even "though already suffering from the ailment which ultimately proved fatal." The next item in the book, a biography of Kerényi that serves to frame the collection, is but a page in length, providing a bare bones, obituary-like timeline involving birthdate and place of birth, date of death, places lived, and career milestones.

Because Kerényi grew up in what would become the Communist bloc (Hungary) and this text is one written from the West in 1984, the biography insists on themes of freedom and intellectual independence. His connection with Jung is mentioned, but nothing is made of his deificatory gloss on Chiron, which to me is perfect. The greatest part of us is always subsumed.

*

Almost all of the pieces in *Essays in Memory of Karl Kerényi* do not focus on Kerényi's work. Instead, they continue his work of scholarship concerning mythology. Kerényi is cited in most of the contributions, but he is far from a central figure. In a way, he hides in these essays, he ghosts them. On the few occasions in which the actual man is mentioned, such as in R. Pannikar's "Yama: A Myth of the Primordial Man," Kerényi appears as a poet-like figure. Pannikar writes that after he (Pannikar) delivered a paper at an academic conference, Kerenyi made a "passionate plea that the term *mythology* may also mean the *legein*, i.e. the telling of the myth, the singing of the story."

*

Bandages staunch, hands clutch. Both can tourniquet, prevent blood from coming out. Wounds welcome these hands and guide them. Apply a salve, or leave to dry. Irrigate. Drain. Debride. Excise the eschar. All listening. Find the right word. What is the kindest thing to say, the quietest? How to hear how I am heard? Chiron, kind father, bless these hands as you have blessed my back and temples, the fields with their blades of grass.

*

Jung returned to the wounded healer idea in what became his last book, a quasi-autobiography titled *Memories, Dreams, Reflections.* He eventually decided the form that would suit the project best would be a more collaborative process in which he responded to questions posed to him by Aniela Jaffé, who then recorded and arranged his answers into a coherent narrative. Jung's theory, then, is enacted: the theory of the "wounded healer" codified by a self-identifying wounded healer (himself) who wished to make sense of his own wounds in the context of his own life, a life devoted to healing the wounds of others. Jung, at the end of his life, made sense of his wounds in the classic dialogic process familiar to therapy. Though the theory found unique expression here, Jung explicitly insisted this was not a scientific work, even instructing that it not be included in his collected works. Jung wasn't being psychoanalyzed by Jaffé per se, but when a genius analyst discourses with anyone, his self-reflection cannot escape both displaying, and even recruiting, his wounds for a purpose. That Jaffé herself was also a psychotherapist, a healer, is worth considering too. For there is no original wounded healer; there is just a long continuous chorale of wounds. You could call this poetry, if you wanted to, didactic heroic pentameters lost to time yet somehow subsumed into poems that recall the beauty of lost songs.

*

In "The Labyrinth," also taken from *Essays in Memory of Karl Kerényi,* Frithjof Hallman claims that Kerényi deals "with symbols in a way beyond the frame of history of art," that he "show[s] us how to bridge the millennia to catch a glimpse of prehistoric man's faith." Hallman does not say that Kerényi is a poet, but that is surely what he means.

*

I speak of Chiron as if he is alive. As if he is in the sky, but also on Earth. As if he still lives, as Kerényi explains he once did, at "a cave on the heights of Pelion."

*

Call my direct addresses skyward prayers to Chiron the god. Chiron, son of mighty Cronos and the Oceanid named Philyra. Cronos, in centaur form, rapes Philyra; Philyra then abandons her son. Consider the import: the wounded healer avatar was wounded at conception, and then again at birth. His wounds precede him then announce him. Chiron is a centaur too, but unique, one with front legs that are human. Chiron, wounded by an arrow shot by Herakles, a poisoned arrow meant for (accounts vary) Elatos. Chiron, whose wound could not be healed despite the renowned mastery of the wound-bearer. Chiron, who lived with his wound for the rest of his life. Chiron, who, as opposed to other centaurs, was calm, deemed a "kind father" by Kerényi, the "wisest and justest of the centaurs" by Homer. Homer also assessed him "sage" and "sire of pharmacy" while teaching the art of healing. Pindar said Chiron possessed "gentle hands in the art of a physician." Chiron, the patient teacher of medicine, first taught the art by his foster-father Apollo; Chiron, the mentor of Achilles, Asklepios, Jason, Patroclus; Chiron, a father figure. Chiron, who, in Jung's formulation, nobly carried a wound that itself contained the source of his healing. From the poison and its permanent effect comes the healing example and action. Chiron, who continues to heal us from the cave. But also Chiron, the god who, according to the myth, eventually died and became a constellation by act of Apollo. Chiron, then, who heals us from the sky. Chiron, the god who yet lives in every single wound.

*

The second fragment from the *Precepts* is in quotation by Plutarch: *Decide no suit until you have heard both sides speak.* The modern version is "There are two sides to every story." For any wound, pain can speak in the early stages. One hopefully moves into a healing stage in which learning can speak and be harnessed for others. Yet no learning speaks unless the pain is respected and given primacy of place, else no healing of others can occur. For unless the pain itself offers its verification to another, there is no point. Who would believe?

*

In the introduction to *Dreams, Memories, Reflections,* Jaffé explains that

> Jung regarded himself primarily as a doctor, a psychiatrist. He was well aware that the patient's religious attitude plays a crucial part in the therapy of psychic illnesses. This observation coincided with his discovery that the psyche spontaneously produces images with a religious content, that it is "by nature religious." It also became apparent to him that numerous neuroses spring from a disregard for this fundamental characteristic of the psyche, especially during the second half of life.

Though a self-identifying Christian, rather than emphasize faith in the face of mystery as a core religious practice, Jung encouraged reflection, and wanted patients to understand themselves in terms of self and world. Only by understanding themselves might they be psychically healthy. During the interview process, Jaffé relates that Jung himself would experience "inner turbulence" that, after some reflection, would spur him into further writing. Jung was compelled to do so because, in his own words, if he failed to "do so for a single day, unpleasant physical symptoms immediately follow[ed]" but if he "set to work they vanish[ed]." Jung sought to clarify his own thinking for himself but also to answer some "objective questions" that others might find of interest. Jung thought through what wounded him, which called him to himself, the he-of-now listening to the he-of-long-ago, responding back as a kind of ongoing correspondence that integrated his health. He demonstrated to anyone reading that it is possible not only to be a wounded healer, but also to heal one's own wounds *as* a wounded healer in the act of wounded healing. Further, his example suggests that one's own wounds should be in a constant process of healing. Health, then, is not biomedical, not the absence of disease but instead thriving (or perhaps just maintaining) in the context of damage.

*

If pain metaphors tend to only be those of bodily damage in English (cutting, burning, ripping, etc.), then in a cosmology of woundedness, it is not the character of the damage that overdetermines meaning, but instead the nature of addressing the wound. A balance can be struck between damage and repair through the waystation of the wound and the way through the waystation, reflection, addressing the wound.

*

In *Fasti,* Ovid writes of Chiron in a way that relaxes my wound. Ovid writes of the "righteous old man" evocatively, that he "is compounded with the body of a tawny horse." The quality of Ovid's mimesis is not the only reason I am soothed. No, I love the representation because of the example Chiron sets. Ovid writes of his death scene as follows:

> Achilles, bathed in tears, stood before him as before a father [. . .] Often he fondled the feeble hands with his own loving hands; the teacher reaped the reward of the character he had moulded. Often Achilles kissed him, and often said to him as he lay there, "Live, I pray thee, and do not forsake me, dear father."

My wound reaches out to touch Chiron's legacy. Chiron the abandoned, who treated young men as carefully as he if were their father; Chiron, cared for to his final breath by Achilles with touch and devotion; Chiron, whose legacy of goodness was the goodness cultivated in his "son." Chiron, may I follow in your example. May I be kind, as you are in myth.

*

The acute sensations: burning, ripping, stabbing, aching; all of these, together, the body in pain. Eight years old with gunmetal in my mouth, sharp hay lacerating my skin, spreading frostbite on my forefeet. Yet other signals frame the damage messages, or rather are the neuromatrix that carries them. The body is alive. The body endures. Some strange words describe the other signals. Though I dispute them, and sometimes spit blood at them. Beauty. Truth. Song.

*

In 2021, I published a poem on trauma, a word taken from the Greek word for "wound." I didn't know about the concept of the wounded healer yet, but my wound sang forth nevertheless in the hopes of sending out a signal of healing, or perhaps in search of same. First, "Fatherhood-Trick" situates pain in the body of my children:

> Point to the place it hurts, I said after your thousand individual, little falls.

I begin, then, as a kind of healer. I am locating the place of the wound, on them. I juxtapose that line with my own pain:

> (I once jumped from the top of an apartment building).

Note that this line is written as an aside, as if within a bandage or cast, something not said aloud, something that shouldn't burden them, but which I carry and know well enough not to offload. Next, I mention an actual clinical anecdote of mine:

> Years ago, a consultant sent a patient back to my office with a note: *Mrs. X says they have "total / body pain." I can't help them with total body pain!*

Such is the judgement offered by a biomedicalist, not a wounded healer, *Be kind* nowhere to be found in the margins. Next, I try to formulate the role of the poem in healing:

> Person as wound? Not the right metaphor. Poem as wound? Too familiar.

I reject the idea of a whole being as wounded. Four years after publication, I still agree. An entire person is not so afflicted. But a poem as wound? Too familiar, but correct because of the commonness. Poems as wounds are our commonality. Still, I am not close enough. I press further:

> Why take a photograph of this for you to see? Poem as wounding.

Yes, again. Poems are a process—of wounding, of leveraging that wound. I make this more explicit:

> In the hospital too long ago, I took a picture of my face as proof of death-in-life. The image displays the selfsame sickness we all must wear, the familiar token—

Here the poem is a demonstration of wounding that is also comparative, shared, ubiquitous, occurring in a mediated, shaped form designed to maximize the power of the wound. I conclude with a return to myself, a recognition of my own need as an acknowledgement I, too, need to be careful since I am in need of healing, no mere expert but a fellow sufferer as I try to be a good father:

> I need a poem that's total-body-pain, I need the selfsame thing

Yet I know there is no such poem, just as there is no such thing as a completely wounded person. Poems are alive, beings—

*

Against protocol, my wound demands I hold space again:

Do not wield woundedness. Bear us (me).

My wound reminds me of the path, the practice. Listen as you fumble along the way. But I do not want to remember, I do not want to listen. I want to wound.

*

In 1972, the Catholic theologian Henri J. M. Nouwen—who in the final phase of his life ministered to the L'Arche community of Toronto – published *The Wounded Healer*, a book in debt to Jung. Although Nouwen's target audience was ministers, the eponymous essay is nevertheless one every physician should read so that they might understand their relation to patients and their relation to themselves. This duality—self and other—is created through woundedness. The modern physician tries to heal the wound by making it go away, by drug and surgery, but healing cannot occur in such a philosophy.

*

As a child, many considered me "broken." As an adult, many still think so. Over time, I've begun to resist the idea of brokenness more intensely. I tell myself that I survived many adverse events in childhood; I survived my own alcoholism, an illness that is understandable, predictable, a survival strategy when considered in its context, in this body; I even lived despite jumping off a building. Do the obstacles and difficulties themselves constitute brokenness? Or am I, somehow, strangely strong? Is *brokenness* another name for *weakness*?

*

The third fragment of *Precepts*, also a quotation made by Plutarch, holds as follows: *A chattering crow lives out nine generations of aged men, but a stag's life is four times a crow's, and a raven's life makes three stags old, while the phoenix outlives nine ravens, but we, the rich-haired Nymphs, daughters of Zeus the aegis-holder, outlive ten phoenixes.* This is nonsense, but a poetic kind of nonsense in which the successive elaboration and perverse precision plays out by image (crow, raven, etc). I could try to interpret the fragment, make a claim that there is a deliberate humbling done of man in the context of the natural and supernatural world, but I prefer to think of the fragment as an incantation, a spiritual precept spoken as a salve is concocted, an elixir brewed. Kerényi is perhaps useful here. Hans Peter Isler provides an insight in his conclusion to "The Meaning of the Animal Frieze in Archaic Greek Art," explaining that Kerényi taught that animal images are "indestructible life."

*

Nouwen sometimes exchanges the term "brokenness" with "weakness." He claims that those who bear wounds are "called to bind [ourselves] with more care and attention than others usually do," that "a deep understanding of our own pain makes it possible for us to convert our weakness into strength." Once this is done, we can "offer our own experiences as a source of healing to those who are often lost in… their own misunderstood sufferings." Restated as a simple equation, Nouwen says something like

Weakness + Acceptance = Strength for Others

This formulation is hardly original—Jung's is a (religiously-inflected) psychodynamic formulation, so is this. Where Nouwen makes an innovation is in terms of insisting on a different definition of healing and a different process. Healing is coming to terms with wounds, and healing others is using wounds to identify and relate. But even more rudimentary is his insight that we, the wounded, are broken. It is no burden to be as if in the margins, whispering *Be kind.*

*

To be Chiron's disciple, one must accept his fate. One must also bear a wound that cannot heal, to always be in the pain process.

*

In "Mythology and Landscape," Hellmut Sichtermann describes Kerényi's theory of art. First, he paraphrases that Kerényi maintained that art "enrich[es]… a whole dimension" and then directly quotes Kerényi as specifying "a dimension of timeless existence." This is, of course, why art often comes from pain, why it moves people without them knowing why. It is the wound as image or oblique word while also being a holding space for the observer, listener, or reader's wound.

*

Nouwen encourages all prospective healers—all of them—to "understand our brokenness." He argues that the wounds themselves are the source of the "healing power" we might wish to wield. By "brokenness," I believe that he means that we exist not in a state of compromised health or spirit, but rather an alignment with the world as it is. We acknowledge that we should strive for harmony with matter, we are immanent, we are not apart. Nouwen does not bring forth the idea of The Fall or any other religious dogma or cliché. Instead, he organizes being under a metaphor of smashedness, splinteredness, sunderedness. I have experienced all of these, either done to myself in reenactment or done to me in the first instance (and all the instances thereafter, forever and ever.) In turn, I smash, splinter, and sunder the lie of normative bliss, converting it into this truth: you, you are just like me. You too are broken.

*

A paraphrase by Quintilian serves as the fourth *Precepts* fragment: *Some consider that children under the age of seven should not receive a literary education.* Meaning, Chiron considers. Our culture considers reading a core competency, a determinant of future success. Statistics bear this out, including a robust finding that children who read have better mental health. My ill father wrote in simple sentences with errors my mother corrected for him. For the first few years of my ill son's life, I read him rhyming books about raccoons, trains, and balloons, but he didn't want to hear, he didn't want to sit, he threw blocks at my hands to dislodge the book. When I turned three years old, I became able to read. I read books I couldn't understand, on purpose. Perhaps this is what Chiron meant. What really am I doing now, I wonder. Why do I continue to seek what I can't grasp—is it some secret of peace, of stillness?—when all that seems to work are fingertips running along bookcloth.

*

Sometimes I stop talking in the clinic, take a deep breath, and reflect on the fact that, in general, I talk too much. I wish then that I could be more like a wound, be wise like one. What would happen if I could simply explain, wordlessly, that I know it hurts, that it is okay?

*

The healer's work occurs by a process that Nouwen explains using the Judeo-Christian concept of hospitality—"the ability to pay attention to the guest." According to Nouwen, attention should come without intent, but with welcome and curiosity; to do this, the healer "must be at home in their own house", meaning that hospitality has the pre-precondition of meditation and contemplation, themselves the precondition of concentration.

Research suggests physicians interrupt patients on average only eleven seconds after we start taking a history. We proceed systematically, inquiring about pertinent associated symptoms. Yes, or no? Yes, or no? Much of this is necessary. The problem comes in the fact that biomedicine does not render unto the human that which is human. The physician who can listen for a time without design, who is curious, is a healer.

There is a second order to the process. Nouwen continues using a house metaphor, writing that the healer gives the guest "a friendly space, where they may feel free to come and go, to be close and be distant, to rest and to play, to talk and to be silent." To do so, an "empty space" must be created "where the guests can find their own souls." Only those "who have come to terms with their own [brokenness] and are at home in their own houses are hosts who offer hospitality to their guests." Our HOUSE as healers must be in order. Our HOUSE must be prepared for others. But when were we (was I) ever at home in our (my) own house? When were we (was I) ever welcomed into that home? The distance between what is for us (for me) and what others need is vast. To bridge that lack, we must literally build our own home to be comfortable in. We must nurture ourselves, offer hospitality to ourselves *before* we can offer hospitality to others. By being wounded, we learn the necessity of shelter, which we can then offer to others by removing ourselves as much as possible, by attending to them, by offering them that which we never had. As Nouwen advises, there is no "wholeness [that] can be given by one to another." Healing is letting people come to learn that fact.

*

Nouwen suffered from a wound like mine. In *The Inner Voice of Love*, a book published just before his death in 1996, he describes his experience of depression. The project was originally not meant for publication, being what has been termed a "secret diary" composed between December 1987 and June 1988. Somehow the process of writing out a daily spiritual imperative worked, and when others learned of the existence of the diary, they urged him to publish it. This book is Nouwen's metabolism of his own wound, a self-reflection buried within, somehow retuning his healing ministry so that he could harmonize with others.

*

Kerényi explains something important, something I fervently believe, in "Labrynthos als linienreflex einer mythologischen Idee," a paper published in *Labryinth-Studien* from 1950. I rely on Hallman's paraphrase, which is: "A secret which has been solved by an explanation has never really been one, as each real secret resists an explanation and cannot be solved rationally." Like Nouwen, I have no real secrets. I publish them eventually. Or, my explanations are partial, broken, small, and can never hope to truly explain anything. In this way, they can never fully *heal* anyone, they can only be *healing*.

*

Don't worry. Anger fades. Your brokenness can never heal because it is a positive state that heals others.

*

A body's first task after wounding is to first create a seal. The gap must be closed, outside must not be allowed in. Epithelial regrowth, proliferation of granulation. An orchestration of cytokines like Epithelial Derived Growth Factor. At night, when I feel a deep ache in my cheeks, or a heavy feeling in my calves paired with a tightness in my neck—as if I am being lifted from the ground, strangled as I try to run—I can let go of the feeling or I can let it let go of me. I look from my window to the constellation Centaurus, but he cannot be fully seen. Visible only from my latitude in this northern country are Theta, Iota, and Nu Centauri. Incomplete representation, incomplete healing. A secret diary. A knowledge of healing, but in part, a submerged Chiron lifting his hands against the roof of my adjacent skin, letting me know that the other part of him is exactly there, that he is working.

I HATE GREAT BIG SEA

No one remembers the day they were born, but I remember the hospital of my birth because I've visited so often. The Oromocto Public Hospital (OPH) is constructed of beige brick. Past the battered parking lot, a senior's residence recedes into a maroon wood finish. A white vinyl funeral home slumps adjacent. The terminal triumvirate, an assembly line of mortality: hospital → retirement home → funeral home. (No one thinks of the hospital as a home.) My mother works at the OPH, and takes me with her when she has no one else to care for me, my little self gleefully shoving over papers when she takes calls in her office, but mostly looking out the window at cars whipping up and down the Broad Road.

Looking out the window, maybe I knew, even then, that I would see a lot more hospitals, that the sequence would be unruly. An ill life criss-crosses them, jumbles them up. My narrative of hospitals would prove to be, at best, a patchwork. Now I must tell you about the other hospitals, of their squat stolidity, their (usually) broken and (sometimes) kept promises of care. What happens in each hospital is less distinctive than location and appearance.

Visit 1, OPH, age indeterminate: a rank of wood falls on my brother's head, opening a small yet exsanguinating cut. Such blood for just five stitches. Always ready for a disaster usually meted out or caused by my drunk father, I escaped the wood tide by ducking behind the big man's legs.

Visit 2, OPH, age eleven: when unsupervised and hoeing a muddy field of cabbage with other children, a frog hops through the pasture. Everyone tries to catch it, but I am the last to realize what the other kids are doing and also the last to try, long after they're done. Besides, it's safer. As I bend over, fanning my hands into a scoop, a strange older boy throws his Rambo knife at the frog, impaling my left index in the process. Corey, my younger brother, always bigger and stronger than me, tosses that older kid to the ground and pulls me to a neighbour's house. Ricky Thompson wraps my finger in an old rag and drives me to the OPH. Five stitches. The tissue soon scars, sensation lost past the flap. What do the doctors and nurses think, given that my mother is the hospital's ranking nursing administrator? Where, indeed, are our parents?

I am still eleven years old. The exterior of the Dr. Everett Chalmers Hospital (DECH) is dirty in 1986, a repellent off-white with a yellow crust on top, a horrible death day cake one bequeaths the sick. Inside is no better: a pockmarked, despotic, institutional blue. One of my nieces had been born, little Jennifer, first child of my older sister. In the bassinet, a baby with pursed red lips and a tiny breathy body swaddled in thick blankets, the only miracle I'd yet witnessed.

Visit 2, DECH, age twelve: my very first time in a psych ward. My grandmother, Sadie, has finally been diagnosed with bipolar disorder and finds herself admitted a short time after her husband, Ralph, dies from a stroke at the OPH. Only a few hospitals in New Brunswick have psych wards, so though the closest hospital was the OPH, Sadie's locked up in Fredericton. Why did my father take me? While we sit on a bench of near-concrete discomfort, another old woman keeps asking me if I would come back again so she could introduce me to her granddaughter. *She needs fixing up!* the old woman says. *She's horrible-hard ugly*. My father thinks this hilarious and responds for me, *Yes!*, elbowing my ribs. Delighted, the manic old woman scurries off to her room to find a picture, some evidence of her granddaughter's homeliness. Looking back with compassion, perhaps it is my father's gift to me that he did go and, even briefly, show his mother that he cared.

Visit 3, OPH, age sixteen: the green rotary wall-mounted phone in our basement sounds a heavy, dull ring. Through the receiver, my mother says, *You've got to come get him, he's embarrassing me, and he'll make me lose my job*! Me: *You mean, he's in the hospital?* Mom: *Come and get him please. It's awful.* When I'm about to say, *What happened to him?* I hear a click. She's gone. I don't really need to ask, though. Something to do with being drunk. When I walk in the entrance, I see Doug being wheeled down the hallway on a gurney. Over my father's drunken shouts, a surly orderly says, *He had a cut that needed to be stitched.* The man's back turns before the gurney stops rolling. Message: we are done with your father. Doug, intoxicated and aggressive, offers mean, obscene ripostes to everyone nearby. *Fuck you and you and you and you. Fuck you twice.* Railroad tracks stretch from his right temple down to his jowl. *I'll take you home*, I say, trying to coax him out of the waiting room and into the parking lot. *Where's that woman?* he says, meaning my mother. *She's at home*, I say, lying. This makes him move. Maybe he can still get her.

Visit 4, OPH, age seventeen: sore throat. Unable to swallow, I walk to the emergency room from a friend's house in town. A francophone physician sees me, one my mother said ran the ER like his family practise, something she hates as an administrator. *Emergency Rooms are supposed to be for emergencies*, she'd say, but whenever she did, I thought of my father slowly rolling down a hallway telling everyone to go fuck themselves. Though gruff and dismissive, the doctor gives me a prescription for sweet, good old penicillin. In less than a day I'm able to swallow again.

Visit 3, DECH, age nineteen: Great Big Sea sucks! A friend from Newfoundland who loves Great Big Sea like it's his country, mother, or lover gets stone drunk in the first five minutes of the collective pre-drinking stage before me and a bunch of other university boys hit Fredericton's downtown. Club Cosmopolitan. Social Club. Cellar. Chestnut. Upper Deck. Dude hits the bottle hard, serially holding countless flasks remarkably vertical at perfect right angles to his lips. At some point, he tumbles out of my capped black Ford Ranger. Chipping his front left incisor, he demands to be taken to an emergency department so that he can see the *fucking dentist* (by this time, everything was "fucking," fucking everything). How he feels about fucking Great Big Sea is how he feels about fucking everything, including his fucking broken tooth – passionately. He rages and swears at the entire waiting room for preventing him from being seen first so that his damaged tooth can be fixed, forcing parents with young children to shoot me dirty looks and demand I make the fucking Newfoundlander shut up. But what power do I have over this fucking acquaintance? I begin to suspect that my friends back at the bar wanted to get rid of him, that I am merely a patsy accomplishing their plan. After three hours of waiting, in which the Newfoundlander sobers up by half, he demands to be returned to where there is *fucking drinking*. When a nurse informs me that the dentist on call says he will only see the Newfoundlander when he sobers up and uses nice language, I know we have to go, for there is no hope of that any time soon, and perhaps ever.

In this love letter, I am not a doctor, displaying neither that experience nor expertise. Consider me instead a person in solidarity with the Newfoundlander who fucking hates fucking hospitals because of what they mean, what they do, and how they work. People go to hospitals in the hopes that they will not just survive, but thrive. In reality, many are lucky to leave, and when they do, they exit lessened, weakened, reduced.

All the other hospitals I've visited as a medical trainee and practising physician clamour in my mind for their turn to be named poetically. They say, *We gave to you, we wish to be included in your litany. Name us.* So I will, though there's little poetry in hospitals, even when relying upon the list method in continuous lineation:

> Victoria General Hospital, Halifax. Health Sciences Centre, Halifax. Nova Scotia Hospital, Halifax. Cape Breton Regional Hospital, Sydney. Saint John Regional Hospital, Saint John. St. Joe's, Saint John. Dr. Everett Chalmers Hospital, Fredericton. Ottawa General Hospital, Ottawa. Health Sciences Centre, St. John's. St. Joe's, St. John's. Miller Centre, St. John's. Dr. Charles S. Curtis Memorial Hospital, St. Anthony. Western Memorial Regional Hospital, Corner Brook. James Paton Memorial Hospital, Gander. Labrador Health Centre, Goose Bay. London Health Sciences

Centre, London. St. Michael's Hospital, Toronto. Western Hospital, Ottawa.

I confess one secret miss, a date I never kept due to illness that should appear on the previous list: McGill University Health Centre. Scheduled to attend an interview for a psychiatry residency, I never arrived. Montreal, as a city, I kept you clean, pure, and beautiful, unsullied by a visit to your hospital, which I cannot hate because I have never been. Perhaps your hospitals are unlike all the others; perhaps, if I visited you, you would cure me of my disaffection.

Visit 5, OPH, age thirty: my mother's Russian Blue cat scratches my three-year-old daughter's face, resulting in the need for steri-strips on her upper lip to approximate the vermillion border. To this day, Zee bears a slight vertical scar.

Visit 4, DECH, age thirty-five: my father needs a CT scan to follow his brain injury. I sit with him to make the process easier for everyone. Of course, it is never easy—he can't hear the television, hates waiting, and is in perpetual need of a cigarette. *In a minute*, I tell myself, *I will be free*. An orderly will roll up with a gurney and take him. Soon I will be alone, experiencing perhaps my only feeling of freedom in a hospital.

Visit 6, OPH, age thirty-seven: I take Doug to the emergency department for a sore arm. Opening and closing hydraulic doors, chattering of other waiting patients, foot traffic of those entering and leaving the hospital, sounds of traffic from outside—it's so loud in the waiting room that if my father had come by himself, he'd never have been able to hear them call his name. He'd have left angry—another invisible victim with "Left Without Being Seen" (LWBS) scrawled on the chart.

I have listed the hospitals as I have known them, as I've returned to them, but I can't stick to sequence completely, for any good story involves analepsis, prolepsis, and the trauma moment as eternal return. So, we return.

Nova Scotia Hospital (NSH), age twenty-seven: old Victorian beast of stone and brick, with gingerbread trim, plaster brackets, moulded spindles, patterned masonry, a stentorian overseer of Halifax Harbour, stern parent of Theodore Tugboat who is visible from the NSH's water-facing windows. Old pipes in the ceiling and single occupancy rooms, a luxuriously sad and old way to live the acute inpatient life. I hear the Newfoundlander say in my head, *I fucking love Great Big Sea* and maybe I do too now, a little? No. I must resist.

Abbie Lane Hospital, age twenty-seven: forcibly held in the Halifax Health Sciences Centre, I hear your rain. As in, how you gave the rain back to me, hitting against solid plate glass that I consider rushing toward, but less so when the rain falls because the sound reminds me of being seven years old and hearing, in the perpetually dangerous place known as home, the soothing sound of water sluicing though tin eavestroughs. Maybe rain hitting your glass on the eighth floor is why I don't die in you, Abbie Lane.

[Undisclosed Hospital Name], 2003 to present day: also a Victorian mix of brick and stone. Why must psychiatric hospitals bear the gravitas of eras—is it because the shiniest hospitals suggest fancy new biomedical cures for physical illness by dint of their modernity, and mental illness requires imposing structures that declare enduringness, sobriety, will? The new hospitals appear slick, mercantile, soulless, whereas old structures contain old ways, are monastery-adjacent in look and feel. Perhaps fifty different wings I walk past thousands of times, all with different British and Scottish names. Intense inpatient treatment, discharge, readmission, a handful of transfers from the Guelph General Hospital ICU. Visits with doctors, groups meetings, recovery meetings, corporate logos floating on the walls. So much of my life spent in your basement, the precise location (Room F) being less a hell than self-subscribing purgatory. Purgatory because though so much of me wishes I were dead, much else of me rejoices that I am not. They say this is the healthy part. It has taken me years to listen and coax out this part of myself, to disagree with the old messages instilled in me since birth, since the OPH where I was born. The old messages: *You are bad, you are worthless, everything you do is wrong on purpose.* I relearned in Room F. In you.

[Undisclosed Hospital Name], 2019: Security Man stands on the entryway's red brick steps. Security Man is new. Security Man has never policed the doors before. People of different ages mill about, smoking on the sidewalk or sitting on broad concrete railings. A small group of women enter after exchanging a cursory hello with Security Man. As I walk towards the entry, Security Man barks, *Patient or visitor?* He's not blocking my path, exactly. I let go of the door handle and turn to answer. But I don't know how to answer the question for two reasons:

1. Autism data drive, torrential thought flow. What, exactly, am I? Long ago, I was a residential patient at this institution. I'm not an inpatient

now, but I still see doctors inside the institution privately... does that still make me a patient? Today, I'm attending a recovery group—does that make me a patient? Am I a patient? Am I a patient? (Am I a retard?) Am I a patient? Should I submit and admit to the security man and say, *Yes, I am a patient?* But am I a patient, or am I not? What is the correct answer? (Retard.)

2. My mind sticks to an image of a medieval gatekeeper asking a supplicant seeking to enter the king's city, *Friend or foe?* Why am I being asked the question? I'm not told. Worse, why must I answer the question in front of people I don't know and who are now watching what is happening? I respond to Security Man, *You mean we have to declare why we're entering the [Unknown Hospital Name] now? Every time we come?* He chuckles, *Yes.* I turn on my heels and walk away, looking back only to notice a group of other women easily enter the building. Why are they greeted at the door, but I am policed?

Later in 2019: It turns out the reason why Security Man policed the entrance that day was because of a credible bomb threat. Yet I have entered and exited hospitals tens of thousands of times, and the predicament I found myself in had never occurred before, with good reason. Nominally, the dispute came because of a need for security of the institution. In its mind, security took priority over consideration of individual privacy. Looked at with both parties in mind, in terms of the practical deployment on the ground, the conflict came about because of stigma. I am male, large, and apparently scary because of size and alterity; hence, to them, I might be the guy who called in the bomb threat. Should the ill and neurodivergent be forced to declare their identities while observed by the public? Security Man could have been discreet. Say, set up a checkpoint and a perimeter, create a somewhat private space for discussion. After being ignored by the hospital despite reaching out to them repeatedly, I petition the Human Rights Tribunal of Ontario for remedy on the grounds of disability. Persisting despite their strategic waiting and lawyer-guided resistance, I win the insertion of a single small clause, three lines only, into their policy documents:

> Upon initiation of the Crisis Response Strategy, elements of the Crisis Communication Plan should be reviewed and implemented as appropriate including considerations for the personal safety and privacy protection of individuals and environmental responsibility.

Because no one on the steps of the [Unknown Hospital Name] or any other hospital has asked me how many times I had entered or exited a hospital, please consider this anti-hospital love letter to constitute my testimony. I want it to be known that, once, you—all hospitals, I hate you all, you stand in for one another, you bleed into one another, French kiss Montreal—tried to force me to declare my identity on your threshold. Threatened with the loss of you, I fought back. You couldn't scare *me* away.

Now you know. Never forget this. There is no way I am going to declare my hatred for Great Big Sea with the whole fucking world watching.

SECTION THREE

NEUROFATHERING

THE NOTEBOOKS OF EVERYTHING IS GOING TO BE ALRIGHT

Every weekday, I walk to my son Kaz to elementary school, a nondescript brick single-floor structure. Small parking lot, unmanageable snarls of drop offs, huge library (but few books), an athletic field that will never get the landscaping love it needs. He doesn't approach any other children, though I encourage him to do so. No other children approach him. Later, when I pick him up from his aftercare, I arrive looking to see if he is engaged with other kids, but each evening he is either crafting with an adult, or he sits alone. On occasion, I've walked past the school playground, looking to see what he's up to during recess. He sits on a bench, by himself, and returns inside when the bell rings. When I ask him why I never see him play with anyone at school, he says, *Because I'm solo, daddy.* After a pause, he repeats: *I'm solo.* Irritated at being asked once more as he nears the end of his time in elementary school, he responds to my habitual question with, *Why do you want me to have friends, daddy?* I think: because I want you to have what I didn't have. I say instead: *Because friends are more fun*. Kaz responds: *But I'm solo, daddy.*

*

At every single meeting with a public-sourced disability professional—behavioural consultant, social worker, occupational trainer—I endure the first five minutes of our meetings as the typical dad, meaning that the women all look to my wife as the primary source of information. Once the five-minute mark hits, I explain that I am the primary caregiver, that I have what they term the "instructional control relationship" with Kaz. Or, as he and I term it: "we're friends."

*

Buster Perley, the intellectually disabled man who lived with my grandparents, loves to sit in a folding chair near the Trans-Canada Highway, spending entire days bronzing in the sun, watching cars and tractor trailers move up and down. The few times I visit my grandparents, Buster extends his hands towards me and mock-undulates his fingers, saying, *I'm going to get you.* I, of course, love Monster Game, and scream while running away. Whenever he sees me later that day, he sticks his hands out again and waves his fingers. Then I disappear again. Eventually, I witness Buster complete his one job at the farmhouse: dishes. His slow body, bending over, standing straight, bending over. My grandparents are paid the lion's portion of his disability pension for his care.

*

I first learn of the existence of the American poet David Ignatow via William Carlos Williams. Devouring everything I can about Williams—his poems, first of all, no small task in terms of bulk, but then moving from there to the autobiography, the biographies, the short fiction, several tomes of letters (god, Williams really let it rip in correspondence), and ending with his criticism—I somehow come across Ignatow, whom Williams once praised in a review in the *New York Times* in 1948, a review that became essentialized in the form of a blurb that came in for a lot of heavy lifting throughout Ignatow's career. The good old pediatrician appreciated Ignatow's writing for self-serving reasons: Ignatow is clearly a (bad) working-class Williams clone. (I celebrate the class element, while insisting on the aesthetic verdict.) My enduring interest has nothing to do with Ignatow's poetry, which I disdain and would warn anyone away from. Instead, the story of his fraught fatherhood continues to obsess me. I think of Ignatow and his disabled son at least once a week.

*

In the Janeway Hospital emergency department, a young male physician trained in New Zealand looks over a new crop of family medicine residents, myself among them. Self-important, invested with grandiose purpose, he wishes to impress us. Short blonde hair, stylish neon red glasses, expensive leather shoes—it's as if he's trying to score while he works. Which, of course, he already did—a young, lithe medical student who he'll sail with around the world. Plus, she's already pregnant. I know all this because of a nurse who punctured his bubble as soon as he was out of earshot. At any rate, Mr. Creep-the-Students stares us down during his initial introduction and says, *If you work here, you need to know something. When it comes to the illness of a child, something happens to parents. They become fighters. You need to know that even if you're dealing with the most easygoing of people, when it comes to their children, they will refuse that which they would otherwise accept.*

*

I am seven years old. My mother teaches me how to fill the dishwasher. She has a system: plates in a phalanx; bowls according to how not to bend the tines. Precise placement of utensils. After every meal, it is my responsibility to clean off the table and deposit dirty plates and cutlery into the dishwasher. I am expected to do this every day, every meal. Back and forth, bending over. Straightening.

*

How am I supposed to show my son how to make friends, how to be a friend, if I myself do not know how?

*

Since the 1950s, the lion's share of research into the parenting of intellectually disabled children has been conducted with mothers. This has only started to change in the past ten years. Initially, the theory guiding research was Freudian: parents typed according to the grief model in *Mourning and Melancholia*. This simplistic view has become vastly more complex over the years, moving to the equational "Double ABCX model" that explains parental stress. In the model,

X = the stress of having a disabled child
A = the specific characteristics of the disabled child
B = a family's resources, internal and external
and C = the family's perceptions of the child.

The "Double" part of the equation means simply that the equation can be run again later as variables change. An open system. Grief evolves, adds, sediments. We have long known that the mothers of intellectually disabled children have poorer psychological health as a cohort than mothers of normative children. Only lately has the finding been confirmed in fathers. Assignation of variables in our case:

> Double = pre-existing mental health diagnosis + grief of diagnosis
> A = Kaz's behaviour, things no one else will know unless they are here, unless they see, unless they are family; things anyone who overhears will discount, or use to blame me.
> B = considerable internal resources but zero external resources
> C = love and fear.

*

When I am eight years old, my father teaches me how to take out the garbage. We use empty old oil barrels, bottoms almost rusted through; the trick is to get the dolly underneath and pull back in a fluid motion so that the barrel won't overturn. Each week, two barrels, Thursday mornings, several terrifying months of screamed instruction before I learn the trick to his satisfaction.

*

The first appearance of Ignatow's son (also named David, let's call him DJr) occurs quite some time into *The Notebooks of David Ignatow*. The reason is perfect: DJr, when in the middle of a psychotic break as a young man, had been loading his father's handwritten journals into a wheelbarrow and dumping them into the Hudson until his father caught him in the act. Journals from 1935–1939 and 1941–1949 all go into the drink. Because DJr was born in 1937, one could think of this action as representative of frustration or anger he bore towards his neglectful father, and there is some basis for this interpretation as corroborated by DSr. But a literary mind who reads the *Notebooks* might come to a different conclusion. Entries from the early years contain dim philosophizing about the literary life, dross that obscures the compelling material that is to come: the story of the Davids. Thus, son David was acting in his father's best interests in a sense, functioning as a ruthless editor, protecting his father from himself.

*

I am ten years old. My father teaches me how to start a fire. It is now also my responsibility to light the wood stove before my father returns home from work in the evening. He shows me how to place paper, what kindling to use and how much, how to place sticks, how to distinguish between hardwood and softwood. Don't overuse paper and kindling. I need to be shown over and over and over again. Over and over and over. Screaming, over and over.

*

Kaz, I say. *That's not friends*. Kaz is harassing his sister, trying to make her cry, claiming that Biggers, our cat, loves him more than her. *Kaz,* I say. *That's not friends.* Kaz rolls his eyes, stomps his feet, and rocks his chair in protest for not getting a treat. *Kaz,* I say. *That's not friends.* Kaz refuses to participate in routines, preferring to sing a song about how he will never, ever do anything but play video games and eat chocos. Sometimes I repeat the rationale: *Kaz, friends are cool and they help each other and they like each other and they get along. I want to be friends. Do you want to be friends?*

*

Statistics concerning the divorce rates of parents of intellectually disabled children are depressing. Though numbers vary, a conservative choice is 80 percent. This figure is absolutely borne out in my personal travels. My son's intellectually disabled classmates are almost all children of divorce. At the dad-of-disableds group I attend, divorce is frequent, but the cohort is heavily skewed to fathers of young children—they still have time to meet their fate. The reason rates are so high is simple: intellectually disabled children, when compared with neurotypicals, have increased rates of behaviour problems, less emotional expressiveness, do not respond to cues in their environment, and have communication issues. Everything is harder, and marriage is hard enough. I stay married because I made a pact with myself at ten years old, standing in the frozen dew after the latest rage of my autistic father. I resolved to fall in love and have a family, for my children to be loved, for things to be different. The little boy didn't think it that way, exactly, for his resolution was more of a feeling, but it has proven a passion that has burnt high his whole life, occasionally roaring higher, should the occasion require it.

*

When I am fourteen years old, I begin to notice that nothing is expected of my brother. He has no chores, no responsibilities. He does not have to clear the table, take out garbage, or start a fire. When I protest, my mother offers no response. *You just have to get it done*, she says when I bring it up. She should have added, "Disablerella."

*

I take Kaz to what we call "Friends School," a Y-based program partnered with the cities of Cambridge and Guelph. There, Kaz makes a small snack, plays a game, and has unstructured time interacting with other intellectually disabled children. When I enter the space to drop him off, we must be careful not to let the serial eloper burst past—a child who flees when the door opens. When I'm inside, another child might immediately try to make friends with me, asking me who my favourite hockey player is, if I know his stats, and if I don't, then how about this player with these stats, or if I know what one huge number divided by a slightly smaller number is, and if I don't, then the answer is… Kaz is welcomed heartily by a smiley young youth worker and bid to come sit nearby, where other children sit, unmoving. I leave with that version of Kaz in my mind: welcomed, walking towards motionless kids.

*

There has always been something between my son and me. Actually, someone. Since Kaz developed a personality at around the age of six months, the energy seemed familiar. Reactive; resistant; defiant; angry; oppositional; violent; insistent; harassing—as if my father's spirit skipped a generation and lodged in my son, so many similarities in temperament and action. But then, who can say that my son is not himself? That I am not re-enacting trauma, distorting our relationship, forcing it through a filter? How can one be a father to a child if one is somehow parenting the child as if it were a violent, neglectful parent? Why be unfair to both of us?

*

According to my father, I cannot do something fast enough, well enough, or at all. I cannot anticipate what he wants. I freeze, making things worse. My brother can easily do what my father requires, meaning that he validates Doug's judgement of my worthlessness. In parallel, my son cannot do what I need him to do. He cannot follow more than a single instruction, and often not even that. He cannot intuit what to do, and if a task requires more than a few steps, he has learned not to try. When he was small, I had a choice. I could terrorize him, break him, make him fear me. I could hurt him. I could do what my father did. Take my turn. But there was never more than just echo, a palsied memory that underlay these encounters with my son. Unlike my father, I dislike acting out anger. I am reluctant to hurt someone else physically, or to be verbally aggressive. It is as if my body brushes off the inclination, the possibility. The only circumstance which provokes this energy in me, in which case I welcome it, stoke it, is when my children are threatened, mocked, or excluded. Then passion rises and seeks release as fury.

*

We sit at a long table in Sunningdale Public School: a principal, a secretary, the teacher, my wife Janet. Me. Thin, gray, and mousy, Teacher's embittered, but her anger isn't with Kaz or us. Before the meeting starts, in an aside with my wife, Teach says, *I've asked for help with him. An EA.*

Something. I've asked several times. Teach is near retirement. Older, anyway, must have just a few more years to go. A cliché runs through my mind: grade one teachers love to work with children. The cliché does not seem true in this case. *Do you think he knows?* she adds. *Knows what?* my wife responds. *Knows that he's different,* she says. A few minutes later, everyone has notebooks out except for us. I reach into my bag, take out a torn strip of paper, and pretend to write things down. Though ridiculous, this gets a reaction. When I start to write, everyone else's note-taking redoubles even though the meeting hasn't officially started yet. The principal, an obese man with a small moustache and heavy, raised moles on his cheeks, says, *We're here to help get Kaz learning where he belongs.* Me: *He doesn't belong here?* Principal: *Oh, I don't mean it like that. I mean, he should be with other people at his level. Otherwise, he'll feel left behind.* Kaz's teacher says nothing. This is, of course, what she wants—to be rid of him. So, I respond directly to her, realizing she was playing both sides all along, *You don't want him in your class?* She opens her mouth, but the principal cuts her off. *It's not like that,* he says. *We want Kaz to be where he can thrive.* Translation: We want Kaz to go somewhere else, to not be here. We can't accommodate him. We won't. Fine. I don't want him here either. But I'm going to cause trouble. Me: *You know she told us she asked you for help with Kaz repeatedly but never got it. A month ago she said the only thing the EAs do in this place is wipe kids' asses.* The notetaking stops for a moment, soon redoubling furiously. Only the principal doesn't return to taking notes. Red-faced, Pickwickian, sweating in a kind of anger, he says, "None of this is helpful. We're trying to help Kaz." Anger and help. Anger and help. I already knew this was never about help, and now I'm more certain.

*

Since the age of twelve, Kaz has learned in a self-contained classroom, meaning he's educated with other children who have intellectual disability. A few months into his first year of high school at age fourteen, I receive a call from his teacher. *Kaz is being taken off work placements*, she says. *He's just behaving too silly. He's too immature for this right now.* The placements involve stocking shelves at a Treasure Hunt and making sandwiches for a soup kitchen in the basement of a Cambridge church. Placements are the apotheosis of his time at Galt Collegiate—the goal is to produce a human who can devote themselves to mechanical tasks for a few hours of the day. Half of the pedagogy is knowing how to take the bus to get to the work site, the other half is doing the actual work. *What's he doing?* I say into the receiver. *It's not bad behaviour, really*, she says. *He just doesn't seem to want to do the work, and so he wanders around being annoying instead. The TAs need to focus on everyone, not just him.* I know what she means. Her tone isn't angry, but fatigued instead. *Kaz will still do work in the classroom, different assignments that will be easier for him because he will remain in this environment, without transitions.* This is the difference between not-help and help, between anger and help vs. sad help. Rather than get rid of him, they work with him.

*

DJr appears in *The Notebooks* as a screaming need, a jolting pain, trial and tribulation. After what I suspect is a prodromal period during his teenage years—progressive social isolation, general disorganization—DJr begins to hear things, see things, believe things. DJr has religious delusions—like me, he can see Jesus. Descriptions in *The Notebooks* are glancing, too thinly episodic, mere shards of clustered anecdotal details; Ignatow still seems like he has a lot to learn about true care and dedication, of dailiness. That said, Ignatow properly agonizes over how he should have paid more attention, how his intensity of affect and resentful attitude towards intrusions upon his writing time partly sponsored his son's schizophrenia. In contrast with scant accounts of care, Ignatow obsessively confesses his guilt. Good confessions connect with the truth, but these feel unseemly, as if guilt is the point, rather than action. The guilt has to be enough for him and for the reader to believe that Ignatow realized he was responsible for his son, finally, in some significant way, that he realized he must respond to the call of his son's psychosis, medication noncompliance, rantings, property destruction, hospital admission, hospital readmission, and, finally, long-term residential treatment at an asylum. We never hear from son David himself, but such is the case with most disabled people. The guilt is not enough for me, as a reader, to believe. For to be a father of an intellectually disabled child in this world is, in the early days, to be an angry helper. Not like Principal or Teacher, but like Father.

*

A's shaking mad, jumping mad, fist up mad, crying mad. His desk's rocking. Stamping mad. Screaming mad. Who knows why, and does it matter? A's angry, he's going off! He needs soothing. In the self-contained classroom, the children do as their teacher, Mrs. Barber, has taught them. In the Barber Shop, students support other students. They try to understand and listen to others. But A is past this point, he's furious. So, the kids do what has been done for them in the weeks and months before. The kids sing their songs to A, to get him to laugh.

Don't worry, be happy
Don't worry, be happy

A settles somewhat. He's still shaking, but spilling fewer tears. The kids bear down with smiles into the next song. They love singing during class—better than math and printing. New song:

Every little thing, it's gonna be alright
Every little thing, it's gonna be alright.

A starts to sing with them, and the kids know that, once again, love has won. He starts to sing too, and when the song is over, A says he lost his purple pencil. Later, B finds it on the cot where any tired child can go and lie down and nap, if they want to. And A wants to, again.

*

Picking up my son at a horse-riding camp open to intellectually disabled people, just outside of Guelph, I overhear an undergraduate age woman talking to another young woman. They both wear blue T-shirts that mark them as counsellors. The tall one: *It takes privilege to treat people badly, I guess.* The small one: *Yeah, the ID kids all seem to get along great. They play with one another. It's the normal kids that are the little shits. They can be so mean.*

*

At the parent-teacher interview for Kaz, his high school teacher says, *We like Kaz. He could talk a little more in class, but it's just his first year. I do think he could be more social, though. For sure. He spends most of his time alone, even during lunch hour.*

*

Since Kaz was diagnosed with intellectual disability, I notice adults with intellectual disabilities (ID) in the community when I wouldn't otherwise, subtle cases like ones taken to Tim Hortons to have a sugary drink by their care worker, or ones brought to the Toronto Zoo. The caseworkers usually gaze at their phone most of the time. Sometimes they seem angry, the disabled person somewhat spooked. The feeling is completely different when I see disabled adults cared for by family: though the parents are older, everyone seems engaged and unhurried. What will happen to my son after I die? Who will take him to Canada's Wonderland, help him negotiate space in a crowd? Will he be relegated to a changing guard of uninvested, paid care workers, transients who could never be expected to actually care about him as I do? Workers who think of him as a case, someone who can be abandoned for an easier, more lucrative gig? Where will my son live? Who will ensure it is safe? Who will fight for him? Who will love him?

*

With the help of a disability worker we've hired privately from outside of the public system, we devise a schedule for Kaz to follow when he returns home from school. First, a snack at the table that he helps prepare. Second, cleaning the table. He must return all the dishes, condiments, and implements to the kitchen, then wipe the surface with a wet cloth. Third, he must sweep the dining room and living room. Fourth, he must clean himself in the shower. All of these tasks require careful assistance. He can get distracted by anything, so each task is subdivided into smaller tasks. Each piece is systematic—start here, move this way, end here. Showering is the trickiest—he is shown how to massage his scalp with his fingers, and to do so we need to use the hand-over-hand method. Move fingers, move fingers, move hand back, move fingers, move fingers. A typical child might implicitly know how to so some of these things; almost every child would be able to duplicate a task after being shown once or twice. Kaz requires diligence and patience, standing beside, sharing the activity in a slow-together way. What would take me ten minutes to do takes him two hours. Redirect. Start again. Redirect. Hand over hand. Start again.

*

This time, it's P. No one knows why. No one said anything. P just got mad. He flicked his tongue against his upper lip, punctuating a screaming sound, tears flowing around his open mouth. But Mrs. Barber knows the answer is not figuring this out, not discovering what's the matter. What's important is soothing P, and to do that, the class must coordinate its care, sing a song. *Happppppeeeeeeeeeeeeeeee,* she sings, but it's too soon for the class to pick up. *Happppppeeeeeeeeeeeeeeee*, she continues. Of all the Change Mood songs, this one is the class's favourite. A few join in. *Happppppeeeeeeeeeeeeeeee, Happppppeeeeeeeeeeeeeeee,* new student recruits coming after each declaration of joy. Once this motor's turned over, Mrs. Barber interjects, *Clap along if you feel like that's what you want to do.* The whole class is in on this now, everybody digging the tune, loving the opportunity to participate in happiness, the happiness level in the room increasing with each chant, happiness made manifest, brought into being. The students with desks around P clap, because clapping is what they want to do. After about a minute, P starts to sputter, then sing the words that, after just three repetitions, stop the tears.

*

What I love about *The Notebooks* is the sense of a selfish man forced into a reckoning about life and poetry. After scores of insipid, self-involved pages simulating insight about the intersection of art and life, the asteroid suddenly hits Ignatow's solipsism, making him realize that there comes too great a cost to leading such an existence. I love also that his transformation is a failed one, at least from where I stand. Ignatow makes it halfway, which is welcome, an achievement, but still a failure to this outsider left wondering if meeting children halfway is ever enough. DSr no longer writes out his ego, thinking only of himself; now a reader can encounter passages like, *I have had a feeling of catastrophe in his life ever since his first hospitalization. He is removed from life and yet has to live a life of his own, divorced from the general life. It is a life of exile and punishment.* Such prose proves Ignatow has changed, he can now partly see his son and realize what has been lost in an empathic way, though solipsism remains (the passage continues, *What has he done to deserve, rather what have I done to deserve his exile?*). Appreciating DJr for who and what he is—that remains impossible. DJr is mostly grief, guilt, and loss for father David. So it was with me too, until I noticed how much Kaz's catastrophe wrought changes in my life that had long been necessary; that my Before-Work needed abandoning and New-Work needed to start, a slow-together work that renovated my relationships with my wife, my eldest daughter, my colleagues – everyone. Worry will never disappear; grief for what might have been for my son may never disappear; but the negative emotion is alloyed with gratitude for being forced to make beneficial changes I would never have contemplated. Just as son David dumped his father's notebooks into the Hudson, Kaz's disability finally convinced me to let go of my desperate wish to simulate normative life. And, most of all: Kaz taught me about fatherhood.

*

Any child out there hurting would want a little platoon of kids singing to them, taking genuine pleasure in the song. With no one afraid of them, no one afraid of difference.

*

Kaz has a friend now in his class. They meet at the local library and talk endlessly about Hot Wheels. How you can get them on eBay. Old Caddies. Dodge Chargers. They play Switch. Kaz rides a scooter to the library and locks it in a religiously careful way so it won't get stolen. Downtown Cambridge is not exactly safe, though safer than the route to McDonalds. He spends hours there, unsupervised, with another human being that is not his immediate family, not someone paid to take care of him. Someone who wants to be friends. And with this single friend, he smashes my personal record.

LIKE FATHER / / LIKE SON

The feeling of being followed is what I remember most. As if there's a legacy I can't escape, a lactic acid ache resting in my arms. Heaviness. Exhaustion. Inescapable demands of care. This is hard, and getting harder every day.

*

The etiology of neurodevelopmental disorders (NDDS) is heterogeneous, including genetic as well as nongenetic factors. Reports of increased rates of concordance for NDDs among twins and family members support a high degree of heritability.

*

In my column "How to Deal" in the *Medical Post* from 2011, I wrote about genetic testing, intergenerational disability, and parenting. I reflected upon whether I would even be alive if my parents had access to testing that could identify my future seizure disorder, bipolar disorder, ASD. I wondered if I myself would have ever had children if genetic testing were available to identify their formidable illnesses—major depression, a rare form of epilepsy that caused encephalopathy. The question I was thinking through back then was, *Is it ethical to have children that will be sick?* As I write in the column,

> No test would have changed my mind. I wanted a child who I could love, and if there were complications to that love, I was prepared to accept them. And now that time has passed and I have suffered the terror of watching a child seize for more than half an hour, and the equal terror of a child who has expressed a willingness to die, I can say with the weight of experience that I was right to become a parent. I have no other life, no other circumstance. Nor do they… There is no genetic test for love. It's trite to say, I know, but really that one true feeling is all that matters. The only family that makes a perfect family tree is no family.

Of course I landed on love as the answer. What else is there? But I have a different question now: *Is love enough?* One answer: *It has to be.* Another response is: *Heaviness. Exhaustion. Inescapable demands of care. This is hard, and getting harder every day.*

*

Just how long is it possible for an average parent to listen? What is an average limit of patience? Of endurance? A reconstructed Kaz conversation, precipitated out here after ten minutes of verbiage: "Daddy I want to grow up and be Marshmallow. I want to play the guitar and be a rock star. No, a DJ. I want to be a DJ and play parties. People will pay me to play their parties. I will drive to their houses and play their parties and they will pay me because I will be a famous

DJ. Maybe I'll eat their pizza. I'll live in a fancy mansion and drive a Lamborghini Countach, twenty-dollar bills in my pocket. I'll do PlayStation all day and DJ at night..."

Kaz, already too close to my face, comes closer the less I listen. Almost pressed against me now, I'm forced to say, "Kaz, enough. I get it. You're going to be a DJ." But he cannot stop. He needs to say more and more and more. He is the monologue in action that tends to stay in action.

"Not just any DJ. The best DJ. World famous. The one everybody hires. You always said you'd be my roadie. Will you help me with my speakers? I'm going to have the biggest ones. Loud enough to break windows."

Despite my warning, he hasn't moved back. His breath on my cheek, his slight unsteadiness making his head rock slightly, every so often brushing against my forehead. "Kaz, move back *now.* Too close!"

When I explain these moments to Normies, they think that the story is merely cute, that Kaz is dreaming in a childish way about adult life. What am I *complaining* about? Their limits are easily reached. But I am not complaining. I seek understanding, empathy, identification that cannot come. The truth is, he won't be a DJ. Not a working one, anyway. For years, he's played the same songs on a free internet program, laughing while madly pushing the arena horn button all the way through. When he plays his Yamaha keyboard, he does so one note at a time, behind the music, on off notes. And he will never, ever drive—indeed, his contained classroom's main curriculum is counting small change and learning how to ride the GRT city bus. I take no satisfaction in recounting his ability level—in fact, I wish his dreams were achievable. Even though I've been with him for sixteen years, I confess I still occasionally fantasize about normativity, the doomed dream he might turn into a *normal* boy and have the *normal* things so taken for granted by most of us. *The normal* amount of *normal* misery. Not this circumscribed, lonely life. In this respect I'm just a *normal* parent, dreaming in parallel.

The DJ topic is merely one of a countless range of Kaz subjects that occupies speech space, that demands a listener, that siphons a finite reserve of attention from an audience. I have sounded these limits in others myself. Normie extended family members hear my attempts to convey the experience of listening to him in bulk, and rather than identify, they defend him instead. "I *like* Kaz." As if I don't like Kaz? As if he needs defending from me, as if I don't need defending from my listener, right now?

Normies hear my stories of parenting an intellectually disabled child and compare them with their own experiences, of the promise and privilege of normative life. They engage in what I call toxic reassurance, a dual censure in which I am told Kaz is able! like! other! children!, that I should not insult Kaz or demean him. *Don't whine about how much work parenting is—of course it's work, you signed up for it.* Normies not only cannot understand, they consider my testimony a defilement of parenting. For they love their children and only speak of them fondly. Yet I ask the cosmos: Who loves their children more than I?

Intrinsic to Kaz and I is a tension. I will be subject to one-sided, vague, and often unintelligible conversations for as long as I am alive, yet I have limits, like anyone. Far more trained, ultramarathonic limits than the normate who might be mildly irritated with their talkative child, yet never admit to it. Only the parents of other intellectually disabled people can understand this burden. Yes, fuck you, *burden.*

*

Modern techniques now result in the identification of genetic etiologies in more than half of individuals with severe GDD/ID, with that number expected to increase with improvements in technology and disease-gene discovery. Therefore, in the absence of a clear and substantial environmental factor that explains the clinical presentation, a genetic workup is appropriate to offer to individuals with GDD/ID and ASD.

*

When Kaz was being assessed for his catastrophic intellectual decline due to a mismanaged seizure disorder, I had to fill out a long questionnaire, as did his third-grade teacher. One question went, "Does the child talk but makes no sense or is hard to understand?" I filled in the "Frequently" circle. His teacher marked the one to the right of that, the circle in the "Usually" column.

*

Again. In my body, arms, the heaviness implanted so long ago. Consider my father, drunk, in the middle of the night, 3 a.m., but as if that image were the experience of heaviness in my body, now, 3 a.m., the same hour I sometimes wake as an adult, short of breath, sweating, touching my sides, asking, "Am I alive?" Only after a few hours of staring out a window can I slowly sink back down into the bed to fall asleep again.

*

My father finally lets my mother tap out and go to bed. She's lasted as long as she can, to the limits of her patience, while he's now screaming and stomping from the top of the stairs. "SHANE! SHANE! GET THE FUCK UP HERE! SHANE!" Then heavy boot sounds tracking back to the living room. Roused from sleep by the drunken summons, I hope he forgets. Sometimes he forgets and passes out on the couch. Instead, he stomps louder across the main floor and shouts again, "SHANE! SHANE!", punctuating every iteration of my name. My name, which through the floor sounds like *shame, shame*. So, I climb the stairs from the basement, sit on the couch, and listen. The long climb, my legs heavy, sleepy, followed by the endless sit.

The feeling is what I remember. Not what he rambles during permasoliloquy, but the feeling: tired, unable to leave, trapped, hostage-*heavy*. Doug could talk for hours, limitlessly. His rambling would lead to anger, for he'd come around to insults and injuries often sustained years before, when he worked on his parents' farm. These would animate him, propel him to more anger. He wasn't treated right, he tried to explain. Not treated right. Every so often, he'd demand a response. "Right?" he'd ask. "Right," I'd say, hating to have to say it, hating to have to listen, hating to have listened for years before I could tell he was spouting nonsense, and hating to listen now that I knew. But as much as then as now, it was incoherent. The pieces couldn't fit together into a story that made sense. The broken pieces made for endless nonsense that made me hate him more.

*

Today I know that my father, during his Epic Drunken Rambles, was looking for the same thing I seek in others: understanding. And I never gave it. I ask the feeling in my arms, "What do you want? Why do I always have to have you?"

Feeling says, "I want you to know everything."

Feeling is like my father: always there, always talking.

Feeling says, "Maybe he didn't know he was holding you hostage. Maybe that's the only way he knew how to be vulnerable."

"No," I say. "That's excusing abuse."

"Maybe," Feeling singsongs. "Mayyyyyybeeee."

"No," I say.

"There's more," Feeling says.

"I don't want to know. Stop it. Go back to just being a feeling."

"It's my time to say no. Imagine how lonely he was, to spout everything he could think of, having no one else to talk to. He was lonely, worried about you in some way, or he wanted to be close to you. He wasn't just using you. In the middle of the night, he was overcome with worry about you based on how he was himself. About how hard he had it and how he knew what was in store for you. So he brought you upstairs the only way he knew how, in a bad way, and held you hostage for hours, ranting."

"Again, aren't you asking me to empathize with my abuser?"

"I really do wonder about this. Both things can be true at once. He was selfish. Annnnnnnd worried."

"NO!"

Feeling says nothing more, resuming its residence as a heaviness felt in both arms, all the way to the shoulder.

*

Parents have many reactions after their child has been diagnosed with an NDD. They often experience acute grief and sorrow over the loss of the hoped-for child, as well as the loss of their expected future. Parents are faced with the prospect of caring for a child through adulthood who may never be able to live independently. Parents worry about the impact on their day-to-day life and finances, as well as impact on their other typically developing children. Parents frequently experience social isolation and stigmatization. They grapple with the question of why this has happened to them and their child, and this often triggers feeling of guilt and blame. Parents may also worry about if they did something to have caused the diagnosis to occur in their child.

*

Kaz's speech requires practice to understand. His lisp and muffle—these the easy impediments. The tougher problem to transcend is threefold: syntactical, vocabulary-based, and attentional. To begin with, his elliptical style of speaking makes for epic jags of sheer saying. He's excited and wants to convey an experience or idea, but it takes a long time for him to get to the core details, or he fails to contextualize the necessary details, meaning one is always piecing together what it is he says, though what he's saying is always at length and often quite rapid in rate. If he doesn't know the word for something, he'll use a vague phrase in its place, or simply default to an "it" or "that" so frequently that a listener doesn't know what the actual referent is. Often, the referent isn't established at the outset, making the reconstruction project impossible. Furthermore, Kaz will regularly skip to the next thing he wants to talk about before adequately sketching the item that came before, meaning one will reconstruct the second item as if it were still part of the first until a listener becomes latterly aware of the transition, by which point coherence is lost and, if energy remains, a listener still interested in understanding, one who hasn't hit a limit, might ask him to return to the first item, asking a series of questions such that the point can be ascertained. Often enough, the point cannot be divined, even with effort. The only other time in my life I've experienced this phenomenon in an equivalent bulk is at 3 a.m. with my drunken father, who wanted to convey everything he felt I needed to know about life through his own disgruntlement and alienation. All the broken pieces that couldn't be put back together again, not like this, and beyond possibility.

*

Often parents attribute their child's NDD to a concrete event or tangible factor, such as nuchal cord at birth or maternal stress during pregnancy. The genetic counselor should respectfully explore these suspicions to understand and appreciate what use they serve, and only when needed, correct misconceptions with information supported by the medical literature. Research has shown that parents accept multiple attributions for their child's condition. As such, they can accept a spiritual cause alongside a biological one.

*

The spiritual cause is that I am

bad.

*

Bizarre to write this now at the age of forty-eight, for I write from memory (there being no record), reconstructing the point of view of a thirteen-year-old. I can't explain the strangeness I feel, for the fidelity of my memory feels much stronger in almost every other circumstance. When I remember something, I remember it precisely, with full colour, verbatim. Here, though, I don't trust myself. There is something I'm missing. Something I don't understand.

Once, my father pulled my brother and I from the back field, took us home, had us shower and dress in the semi-formal clothing we only wore to rep hockey games. "We're going to the Boat Club," he said. The Boat Club in Lincoln, New Brunswick, was renovated in the early 1990s so that it could function as a social club and not just a launch. The first signal of a memory glitch, of unreliable detail, comes next. A maître-d (there would be no such thing there at that time, more like a manager, perhaps, or a front server) inquired if my father were a member. "No," Doug said. "I'm with Bill. I'm his guest." A legendary Bill? Bill whom everyone knows? Apparently, since we were permitted entry. Members, I learned, could bring one non-member at a time to the club so long as the member was present. The dining area offered a few scattered wood tables, their scarcity serving to amplify the effect of the room's obvious centerpiece: a huge oaken bar. Men in business suits sat at the end, talking amongst themselves; one of them was Bill. I heard the men say his name repeatedly. Bill, the only man with a name, never said theirs. We sat down, too, even though my brother and I were much too young, but at the other end of the bar. Bill didn't acknowledge my father immediately. After a few minutes, Bill either noticed him for the first time, or decided to approach after pretending not to notice him. He came over to talk.

Bill. Bill Bill Bill.

It strikes me as another strangeness now to note Legendary Billy had the same first name as my father, William. A name my father had somehow lost in favour of his middle name, Douglas.

"Hi, Doug!" he said. "I came over after you called—got here fifteen minutes ago." With a mischievous smile, he added, "Left the wife with her G&Ts." They talked about work for ten minutes or so until more people filtered into the room. All of them knew Legendary Billy.

Bill. Bill Bill Bill.

Somehow Bill got pulled away, back to the other end of the bar where the business suit group grew bigger and more boisterous. "Left the wife with her G&Ts," he said to laughter. And again to other people, to more laughter. I heard him say, in a neutral way, "That's Doug Neilson." Did someone ask him who the guy with two kids was?

In time, we moved from the bar to one of the tables and sat there, my father ordering drink after drink, no full bottles for sale. Bill, the only person who'd talked to him in the entire place, was gone. I didn't feel like my father was being ignored by the suits on purpose, certainly not shunned. My memory tells me that he just didn't fit. Doug came from a country farm. He was a high school dropout without a GED, let alone a university degree. Here we were, which meant he wanted to fit this place, to be of it. The bartender kept serving him drinks. If the management wanted him to leave, then they would have cut him off. The crowd thinned out. Either no one knew my father, everyone knew *of* my father, my father didn't have the skills to make friends, or my father felt out of his social class. That, or everyone was uncomfortable with the prospect of a father getting drunk in public in front of his sons, my brother and I the only two minors there. When Doug ran out of cash, we left. I drove home.

I do not trust these details. Something like this happened. But recalled details are a form of interpretation. Something is here I do not understand. Even though I do not understand, I identify. Perhaps this is it. For maybe the first time in my life, I could sense his loneliness.

*

An irresistible compulsion: I walk past my son's school during recess. At random, I stop what I am doing and I make River Oaks ten minutes later, approaching from the back, using a city trail to enter the park. I don't need to get close. I know where to look. Children move chaotically in the foreground, large groups of them, pairs, triads, a flurry of multicoloured balls. Sure enough, in the background I see Kaz sitting on a bench near the school, by himself. Kaz looks down slightly, unmoving. After just a few seconds of this, I cannot look, so I return home to sit by myself, looking through the window out onto Pen Street's non-drama. Is there a spiritual cause to all of this? Or is genetics all? What is genetics but another word for destiny?

*

It may also be helpful to reassure parents that all available testing has been pursued and an exhaustive search for information has been performed, and then the genetic counselor can assist them with coping with the residual uncertainty, stress, and related challenges of caring for their child with NDD. Genetic counselors can use interventions that aid parents in using more effective coping strategies.

*

"Daddy, I want Frink. Can we go get Frink? I've been Good. I'll be Even Gooder. When I'm Even Gooder, can we go get Frink?"

"Kaz, we get Frink on Mondays, after garbage. Tuesdays after a long weekend."

"But I've been Good! And you're always saying Be Good. I'm Good now! And Good means Frink. You said."

"Kaz, just ten minutes ago you kept poking your sister and made her scream. We told you to stop but you didn't."

"I'm Good now though!"

"You're Okay now. I like Okay. Lets stay Okay together."

"No. Good together. I want Frink."

*

Several times a day, this: whether to go or not to x, y, and z.

X, y, and z are activities, excursions, opportunities, rewards, ceremonies. Attendance is dependent upon the Behavioural Coefficient (BC), which adjusts probabilities up or down. If BC's poor—e.g. general or directed aggression, targeted antagonism, destruction of property—then the decision to invest in the effort to attend an activity might seem obvious to a normative parent. For the Normies, one cannot incentivize behaviour one does not want. But to levy this rule with iron consistency would be foolish, otherwise several times a day, this: not going to x, y, and z. And after a regroup, not going to a, b, and c. We'd cycle through the alphabet again and again. We would go nowhere and do nothing but suffer more of the behaviour, with none of the learning that occurs in a normative child when denied their desires. But the dialectic: to go to the activity is to have the normative advice nag every second, often in a misalignment, parallel with the reality, Kaz's poor behaviour persisting throughout the activity. The Normie parents aren't wrong. They're also not right.

I see this as being taken hostage: damned if I do, damned if I don't, stuck at home or stuck trying to make something work that won't. That can't.

"Do you think you are just repeating your trauma with your son?" asks Dr. J.

"I wish it was just me," I answer. "But they both do the same things. They talk the same way."

*

Research has shown a relationship between hope, uncertainty, and psychological adaptation. Hope can be conceptualized as a cognitive process that is comprised of a sense of agency (goal-directed determination) and pathways (planning of ways to meet goals.)

*

Is the heavy feeling in my arms hope? "Hey, feeling. Are you a kind of hope?" Feeling doesn't want to talk.

*

"You know the thing on YouTube? The thing was really funny. In school today they said the thing wasn't real, but I said it was because we saw it together. You know the thing, a chip right? It's a chip for computers. But that won't work on it. [A classmate] says he has one but I don't believe him and anyway he always says he has stuff. I said show me on your phone but he didn't. The YouTube just came and I lost it so I don't remember the name of the thing but I showed you right? Mrs. M. said it's epic and they did too."

"Kaz, what thing on YouTube?" I am a perpetual Jeopardy contestant.

"Well, it was red and it made a noise, I don't know what to call it. But it's cool."

"What is it used for?"

"I told you. Computers. If I had one then I could do my work a lot faster at school but Mrs. M. says even though it sounds good I have to do my work myself. But I think it's accessibility."

"Kaz, do you mean ChatGPT?"

"I guess…"

*

I call a friend from within the locked unit of [Undisclosed Hospital Name]. She accepts the charges collect. Talk turns to my father, who's recently sustained a critical head injury. I want to feel good about myself, to tease out a distinction between him and me that is to my credit. "I'm here in the hospital on suicide watch. Took a whole bottle of Clonazepam, but at least I don't hurt anyone. At least I don't enjoy hurting anyone else. At least the damage I do is only to myself. At least I'm not like my father."

She responds, "Depression is hate turned inward. Not really so different."

*

Meaning-making is a key component of the adaptation process. In a study of family caregivers of individuals with developmental disabilities, researchers have found that identifying positive meaning in caregiving was a strong predictor of caregivers' subjective well-being. Genetic counselors can facilitate a discussion with parents about their experience of being a caregiver and encourage them to tell their story, verbally or through a writing exercise.

*

It was me, I did this as link in the chain. I am

bad

*

"I want Frink."

*

The heavy feeling, it is hope also—

*

We are on the cusp of precision medicine for individuals with NDDs. ID and related disorders have always been considered incurable, with treatment instead focused on symptom management and therapies to support development. Genomic advances have led to an increased understanding of the pathophysiology and neurobiology of NDDs, and it is expected that this will eventually lead to targeted treatments based on underlying genetic etiology.

*

My father wants me to take him to the Canadian Tire. He wants mulch. He wants a replacement hose for his dishwasher. He wants to load up on driveway salt out of season. He needs to go now. He needs it now. Now. Now. Now. Take. Now. Now take now. Take now. If he doesn't get the salt, then it will be sold out. It's a good price. He asks if I want some to take back to Ontario, even though I flew out to see him, he forgot to pick me up at the airport. Mulch now because the front garden needs to be ready. Ready now. The dishwasher isn't broken but he thinks it might break. It broke a few months ago and he doesn't want to be hung up again. He watched the repairman fix the problem and kept the broken part. Maybe it will break again. He needs to be ready. Ready now. I turn to him, me on the La-Z-Boy, legs up, feet humming, him on the extra-long leather couch he uses as a bed, his circumference of daily life so small now, this couch and the coffee table ahead, pock-marked with knife scrapes, cigarette burns, smeared ash, and loose coins. I turn to him and say, *You sound just like my son. I thought I would get away from this one day, but I haven't. It's followed me. You followed me.* But Doug doesn't care, compelled to be nothing but himself, existing as nothing other. All that matters is that I do what he wants, give him what he wants. Now. We need to go now, he says. Now.

NOT THE SMARTEST

Part One: When Blameless

When small, I have a single exemplary ability: I am smart. No one is as smart as me. No one.

My father: *You're stupid. A retard. You're fucking dumb. You're such a fuck-up. What's wrong with you? Why are you so slow? Why don't you know how to do anything? HEY! Fucking hurry up! Idiot. Moron. Shit for brains. Dumbass. Retard. Retard. Retard. Retard. Retard. Retard. Retard.*

Retard? Why can't I accomplish basic tasks that others seem able to do? Things my brother, for example, can naturally do, like know what end of something to hold, where to stand, or how to use a tool. The generic interactional structure of my brother helping my father in the garage or a field or anywhere on earth:

(a) My father needs something.
(b) About to ask, my brother anticipates the need and has that object ready.
(c) Magic.

(d) My father needs something else.
(e) My brother already has it in his hand, too, giving it before speech is even required.
(f) Magic.

An endless set, simple arithmetic I can't add up: {a} + {b} + {c} + {d} + {e} + {f} = normativity. Me helping my father anywhere on earth:

(a2) I'm staring at a dust mote in the sun.
(b2) All the motes are oddly forming a pattern.
(c2) A shout: *Get the fucking*
(d2) *Why don't you fucking*
(e2) *Did you fucking hear*
(f2) *Why the fuck you fucking stupid fucking*
(g2) Run.

I have a praxis issue, a difficulty understanding how to move or what to do in the world of men. What is space, moving through space? Do other people think about how to move through space, or do they just do it? When my father needs a hammer, I wonder what light is, how it could be a thing, not astrophysics or solar bodies or nuclear reactions but rather a phenomenology of light. From a particular way of thinking—survival, say—this *is* fucking stupid.

A host of perpetually refreshing bullies:

You're stupid.
A retard.
You're fucking dumb.
You are such a fuck-up.
What's wrong with you?
Why are you so slow?

Why don't you know how to do anything?
Fucking hurry up!
Idiot.
Moron.
Shit for brains.
Dumbass.
Retard.
Retard.
Retard.
Retard.
Retard.
Retard.
Retard.
Retard.
Retard.
Retard.
Retard.
Retard.
Retard.
Retard.

Retard?

Mom, 2010: *You were gifted, but I wanted you in regular school so you could socialize like normal kids. I thought that was important.* She and I never talked about how odd I was (and remain), of what it was like to be a mom to a neurodivergent child who was never identified as such. Wait, did she mean "gifted" as in smart or as a euphemism, as in "special"? As in, "retard"?

The larger world considers me a retard. Retard at Beavers, at Mites, at church. At school, especially. When teachers grow tired or frustrated by the apathy—okay, I'll just say it—of the actual stupidity of my classmates, the teachers call on me, and I answer them correctly. When tests are returned, I'm first in class. This constant superior performance goads bullies. I grow into an objective awareness of being smart, so bright that no one else in my young life ever comes close. As larger and larger classrooms come with time, I continue to be the smartest—by far. Bullies hate that I command the correct answers. I own them all. For them, I am the smartest stupid fucker they would ever meet, an intelligent reject shithead moron Rain Man retard.

Part Two: Monkey See, Monkey Do

I am actually not the smartest, as you already suspect.

Age nine: looking at the special education kids sitting in their wheelchairs outside Hubbard Avenue Elementary School and thinking: *I want to throw rocks at you. You are the retards.* Only now do I understand that I hated them because I was equated with them, I was called what they were, and in a more profound shame, I knew I wasn't just like them, I was one of them.

Age twenty-four: my non-neurotypical father falls from the top of a semi-trailer, taking such a Humpty Dumpty that he develops an intellectual disability to compound his other problems. At the Stan Cassidy Centre in Fredericton, he's taught to use the bathroom again, how to write and walk again. From the age of fifty-five until his death at seventy-four, he requires a live-in minder—my mother—to care for him. He's now *her* gifted one, re-gifted to her. A week after he comes home, he says: *There's nothing to live for. I can't do anything anymore. I'm useless.* Thinking of all the times he's called me shit under his feet, nothing, worthless, stupid, useless, so fucking stupid, stupid on purpose, I might agree with him.

When the abused become independent adults, the tables can turn. I perform a routine every time I call my father on the phone. Every single catchphrase and repetition, every one of his phrasal ticks, is purposed into my parodies.

Doug, about something: *I guess I forgot.*
Me: *How can you forget what you never knew?*
Doug: *Ha, ha, ha. Good one.*
Me: *I've done more forgetting than you ever knew a goddamn thing!*
Doug: *Ha, ha, ha. You're a funny one!*
Me: *I've forgotten more roads backing up than you ever drove remembering, frontwards! Goddamer. Hellew!*

Given the opportunity by the gods to get free and clear, to be redeemed, to forgive, I recapitulated the past rather than let go because it was *my* turn, *my* chance to dominate. Not the smartest.

Age forty: we drive to the Dr. Everett Chalmers Hospital ICU as my mother suffers the illness that kills her.

Doug, in the passenger seat: *Babble, babble, yak, yak, prattle, babble, yak, beg, wheedle, whine, babble, yak, babble.*
Me, in the driver's seat, clucking like a chicken: *Buck, buck, buck, buck, buck, buck, buck, buck.*
Doug, repeating his worry of the moment or small concern: *Babble, babble, yak, yak, prattle, babble, yak, beg, wheedle, whine, babble, yak, babble.*

Me: *Talk, talk, talk, fill the space with words, havta talk and talk some more, talkity, talkity, talk, talk, babble talk.*
Doug, about to babble again as if I am there to help him, to answer, as if I am good, his son, but I pre-empt him with, *Talkity!*
Doug: *But—*
Me: *Talkity!*

Part Three: My Shame

Me, to Kaz, age four: *Kaz, that's stupid! Kaz, that's dumb!*

Stupid.
Dumb.
Stupid.
Dumb.
Stupid.
Dumb.
Stupid.
Dumb.
Stupid.
Dumb.
Stupid.
Dumb.

Kaz: *Can I tell you something about my day?*

Clinical psychologist: *Kaz is intellectually disabled at a mild-moderate severity. His intelligence is at a level that's below 1 percent of the population. You can think of some of his behaviour problems at least in part as an understandable response to not understanding his world.*

It takes privilege to be a bully. If I invoked the context of the behaviour problems and the exhaustion of parenting a disabled child, would my behaviour be excused? What about considering my personal history in which I was conditioned as a "smart retard"? I know. Smart people need no excuse, have no excuse. Parents of disabled children must be saintly. Normies require perfection and a tidy sequestration of the problem within the domestic space.

Often Kaz doesn't make sense. His stories aren't intelligible. I pride myself on my ability to tell complex, emotionally-layered stories. Kaz often grunts and acts menacing when he doesn't get what he wants. He hits his mother, he harasses his baby sister. Am I pathologizing him now? He has no voice, and I do? Don't worry, I'll focus on my part: smart people have no excuse and need none.

Such heaviness in my body, solidifying to speak:

You are not the smartest.
The one gift we gave you, you use as a weapon against your own family, even though you know this is internalized ableism.
Don't say that you are trying to stop!
You know that the urge, the impulse, will always be there!
Because when you were small, you were hurt? So what. You are not the smartest!

This part completes the story. At last. At last. I have described the ugliness.

MCDONALDSING INTO THE FUTURE-DEATH

We call it Frink, and Frink it has been since he was able to demand "drink." Frink it remains, though Frink is specific in a way only his family can know: a carbonated drink from McDonalds as dispensed by an accessible self-serve fountain (a pox on behind-the-counter tyrannical control!). Though cup sizes have escalated over the years, Frink's always come as an earned reward. Frink as the meaning of life; Frink as the purest joy; Frink as the promise at the end of a long day pining for Frink; Frink if, and only if, one is Good. Frink *because* he is Good. Consider Frink to be your sex, your drug, your rash internet purchase, but also your wholesome chaste handhold with a first date at a carnival, your sleep stuffy, your comfortable around-the-house lived-in sweater. Frink for a blissful, refill-laden hour. Then the return to normal Frinkless life.

*

At the Toronto Zoo, a spooked, middle-aged woman walks alongside a much younger, frowning woman, their age difference thirty years, at least. Woman the Younger seems in a hurry; Older moves in a way I know: slow, subtly uncoordinated, arms slightly flexed. Her clothes (pastel polyester pants, an unflattering white blouse) fit poorly. Her thick, slightly sticky hair is shaped like a hard hat. Ungroomed, not unsightly or unkempt. In contrast, Younger dresses stylishly, in an actual dress—Van Goghian, blue with yellow erupting sunflowers. After a few more seconds of observation, I realize that these two probably unrelated people—they are different races, there is no affection—have been brought together in a care relationship. Older, who's intellectually disabled in some way, is being led by hand-pull, not hand-hold. Ah. Like my son, she can't move any faster, it seems. She's not resisting, she just lacks a faster gear. Younger the Frustrated wants to get somewhere. Always, an abled somewhere to hurry to on the way to another Important Place. Older could be fearful about anything, I suppose. To be fair, Younger could want to get elsewhere for any reason, perhaps a reasonable one. In my gut, though, I interpret this scene as a disabled person taken out on an excursion by a personal support worker, easy gig for them. The relationship is both paid and overtly uncaring. It's happened before—I sense Older accepts the lack of concern as the cost of coming to the zoo. I ask you: when you were a child, unable to arrange a trip to McDonalds, the movie theatre, or the zoo on your own, wasn't it enough to just go? When I turn my head to see if anyone else notices the pair, I witness everyone else involved in their own lives, couples and families, my own son and daughter fighting over who saw the first polar bear. Kaz says "Me!" Aria says, "No, me!" I wouldn't come here if I didn't love them. I wouldn't take them if I didn't love them. I am privileged to love them. They are privileged to be loved. Is that right? That shouldn't be right.

*

Kaz is late for the special van that couriers him and a few other disabled children to Galt Collegiate. By this point in our lives together, my self-appointed job title is "Leaving Specialist." From the time he entered kindergarten until now, a strong organizational structure conveys, coerces, and coaxes Kaz to leave the house in the morning. First, music from downstairs. Then, I climb the stairwell and call to him from his doorway. (Lately, he picks his own clothes.) Then, breakfast after he removes his Invisalign. Breakfast's intricate movements: for the past few days, he's attempted to choose an item or two from the fridge. Item choice influences pacing because peanut butter takes minutes to spread on crackers, an apple thirty seconds to slice. Breakfast is carefully arranged—he gets a halfway warning, a five-minute warning, and then an absolute final warning to leave the table and dress for outside. Ding, louder ding, loudest ding. Waiting by the door, of course, are his bookbag (packed with a lunch made by his mother that he won't eat, but which we must pack or else the school will call us to bring one he also won't eat), coat, and boots. I have streamlined everything, economized all. Milk in the fridge stands ready to pour, his go-to foods always accounted for and facing frontward, otherwise the routine will be disturbed, Kaz will angrify, and his chances of catching the bus reduce. If we fall behind, there is but one absolute truth and certainty: he will not, cannot accelerate. The factory installed a single low gear. If we fall behind, no admonishment can quicken him. This deep understanding of intellectually disabled physics enables me to discern the nature of care relationships in the wild. When I encounter ID people in public, I watch their carers. Are the carers in a hurry, at odds with their charges, or in synch? My son may never know this until the day I am gone, but the fact that much has been cleared away for him, that preparation and expertise smooth his progress, is a mark of love through action. Love is also that I understand he cannot be made to go faster, that slowness is his nature. If I were to shout and scare him as I was myself so often scared as a child, then he would startle, yet not move faster and quicker. And when I see him startle, I see myself, and I never want to see myself that way again, too scared to even move. Too heavy to move.

*

At the Toronto Zoo, I order an iced lemonade for Kaz and a croissant for my daughter Aria. Kaz savours the liquid, nursing it for over an hour; my daughter gobbles the croissant. Next to the entrance to Africa Savanna, Kaz sets his lemonade down on a concrete railing and tries to locate the biggest lion, but they hide from the sun, undetectable. When he turns back to his lemonade, yellowjackets swarm the rim. He looks up to me, asks me to get them away. Though I'm not scared of being stung, I know that stinging will happen with so many wasps crawling on the top, several already past the straw aperture soon to reach the sugar water. Plus, he shouldn't drink the thing now that the wasps are in there. Plus, I want to teach him to respect danger. So I say "Let's leave the juice for them. They're yellow. It's yellow. Yellow things go together." But he does not accept my silly reasoning and begins to rage, screaming about his Frink, how it's his, how he should still have it, noowwwwwwwww. The meltdown continues for another thirty minutes. The lions refuse movement, too.

*

Two women sit across a coffee shop table from a middle-aged man. He smiles oddly, askance from them both. Only one woman speaks to him, often in a singsong voice about his "treat." Every few minutes, she asks, "Do you want your treat?" Each time, he nods in return, says, "frozey lemonade," while continuing to smile. The one that doesn't speak to him continues to not speak to him. In a minute, the one that talks to him leaves the table, soon returning with a yellow semisolid liquid in a large plastic cup that she places in front of him. The one who doesn't speak to the man mentions her previous night spent with a boyfriend and how much of an asshole he is. Apparently, he's handsy and cheap. The one who singsongs to the man responds with a generic sympathy no more authentic than her singsong interactions with the man. Now it's her turn to talk, and she describes an aggressive client, pausing only to coo to the man who smiles oddly, who is not aggressive, no no, he is good, good. She talks to him like a dog. Then she complains about another client who soils himself and needs constant watching, otherwise he'll run away. The one who doesn't talk to the man mentions how much she hates her ex-boyfriend, who always walked around the house naked. Though she didn't exactly hate how good he was in bed. The singsong woman watches the liquid level in the smiling man's cup, as I do: the meniscus vibrates slightly as trucks rumble by the drive-through window. How often does the group home send someone to take him here? How often does he get his treat? Is treating the only activity he does outside the home? Is there anyone to love him?

*

A detail only a parent of a child with intellectual disability could understand: Henry Lee Lucas, a serial killer who died in custody in Texas, confessed to many dozens of murders he didn't commit because his parental figure, thin Jim Boutwell, a paternalistic Texas Ranger (white Stetson, unfiltered Lucky Strikes, cowboy boots, handcuff tie clip) allowed him special privileges. According to records, Lucas had an IQ of 85, yet in watching him, I see my son's same slowness, ID speed. In some respects, an IQ of 85 is a world away from 70. With 85, one can do well enough to get a driver's license, work trades; at 70, my son's IQ, the likelihood of passing the driver's test is miniscule and employment is largely subsidized by the state through agencies. Maybe it's the way Lucas holds a milkshake, as if it doesn't matter where he is, what will happen to him. What matters for Lucas is that, right at that moment, he's got a milkshake in his hand. Footage exists of Lucas ranging freely within Boutwell's jail, sucking on a strawberry milkshake. Henry Lee Lucas, a Frink for every murder confession that clears a capital case.

*

From the time he could walk, Kaz helped me take out the garbage. Once a week, we used to drag the blue, grey, and green containers streetside. Early on, he play-helped, but even when he contributed nothing except trouble, running underfoot, chucking Frink containers out of the bins, overturning the bins, and shoving bins onto the street, I considered this activity his "job" and he would be rewarded with apple juice after we finished. As he became older, repetitively shown what to do week after week, year after year, and given so much juice, he eventually became able to perform the task himself. Once he completes a cycle (garbage out in the morning, bins back in the evening) correctly, without cueing, then the reward comes: a trip to the McDonalds on Main. Frink, from the fountain, classic mix: two-thirds Nestea, one-third red Fruitopia. The visit has its own ritual: we try to sit in the same place in the restaurant, across from the fish tank. We locate the sucker fish who hides in the hollow tree. We look for anyone else disabled. I don't say what I often wonder: who will take him to McDonalds after I am dead? I know the answer already. Either *no one*, or *people who don't care about him*. After a refill, we leave.

*

At Diwa in Guelph, a waitress places curry rice on the table. I'm having lunch with a physician mentor, a middle-aged woman with high risk tolerance for unfamiliar medical situations. A natural leader, warm and inviting—all things I am not. She knows about Kaz, has long known. For the first time, she discloses why, perhaps, I like her so much. "I have an autistic person in my family," she says. "I had to take care of him a bit when I was an adolescent. We used to play bouncy ball, he'd do that for hours, chuck the ball in the house and then go find it. His mind just worked differently. Then one of my sons was born non-neurotypical and I played more bouncy ball. My life has seen lot of bouncy ball." She says the words bouncy ball like she's one of us, as if chanting them in singsong gives infectious pleasure, as if a roomful of children would suddenly become delighted repeating "bouncy ball" to one another, as if the words were the ball and we had to make the words bounce. As if the words were proper nouns, Bouncy Ball. No, as if the words were all caps, BOUNCY BALL. As if every phoneme were an exclamation mark. "One of the things I hear from my patients and friends who have disabled children is that they fear what will happen when they are gone. They tell me that's the worst thing they have to think about." Ahead of me sits my glass of water without ice, never ice—I despise the sensation of ice on my teeth. The meniscus rests, unperturbed. I could climb in and swim.

*

Another restaurant, this time Mandarin on King Street in Kitchener. Mando is Kaz's favourite—he can see all the buffet items and pick exactly what he wants. Fries, onion rings, gravy, and California roll sushi, an undeviating selection. Everyone else at the table—Janet, Aria, me—drink water, Aria with double ice because I spoon out mine and make the exchange. Kaz gets iced tea. Across from us, a disabled pair of young men sit at a small rectangular table. One of the men is dressed as life-size Super Mario, red cap, suspenders, the whole deal. The other man has pronounced retrognathia and strabismus. I hear a speech impediment, a heavy lisp but also dysphonia to boot. As I eat my undeviating meal, chicken fried rice and chicken balls, I map the dynamic between them. Super Mario makes several trips to the buffet, his heaping plates scarfed down and replaced with more. He's genial, always answering "Yes" to the other's pleas to hang out after dinner, to hang out at other times. "Let's hang out later" says the pulled-back jaw man after perhaps the two-dozenth "Yes" to the same question. It's unclear if the man has been stood up or ghosted by Super Mario before, or whether his anxiety reflects being ignored by others. He pulls out his phone and shows Super Mario something. Retrognathia giggles, Super Mario guffaws. "Isn't this fun?" Retrognathia asks for the tenth time, adding a new variant, "This is so fun, isn't it?" As per the ritual, "Yes" comes as response. In time, the waiter comes by, asks "How are you going to pay?" in what I deem a not un-nice way, a not-mean way. A regular way. The normal way. Super Mario points wordlessly to Retrognathia, who volunteers that he will pay. I can tell that this was the deal. Retrognathia's credit card doesn't work on tap, so the waiter inserts it into the machine for him, but Retrognathia doesn't know his passcode. Retrognathia calls someone on the phone, places it on speaker. Someone I assume is his mother patiently recites his code over and over again, a code for a card that is quite possibly hers. The code doesn't work even when the waiter puts in the numbers. The waiter looks to Super Mario. "Can you pay?" he asks, but Super Mario smiles and says that he cannot. "Can your parents come and fix this?" he asks both of them. Have they been here before? Does he know they have parents? Realizing this interaction is attracting a lot of staring, the waiter commands the two men to stand up and move to the front of the restaurant where the manager will "work things out." When I finish eating ten minutes later, I walk past the two men sitting at the front. Super Mario stares ahead happily. Retrognathia talks down into his phone, an image of an old woman looking back at him.

*

Excerpt from *Shane Neilson's Imaginary Last Will and Testament, as Written on a Brown McDonalds Napkin Using Red (Provided) Crayon*

For my son:

1. Frinks, once weekly
2. Spotify account

3. Gorilla stuffy, medium size
4. Computer with GarageBand
5. Someone to love

*

In the hopes that Kaz can be Frink-autonomous, Frink self-sufficient, beFrinkable, I send him walking up the kilometre-and-a-half incline to the McDonalds on Main Street. A quest for Frink. Money's pre-loaded on a card, and we've practiced (and practiced and practiced—after all, we come here every week) using the very accessible touchscreens that print out a ticket he can use to pay the cashier. Two hours later, he bangs on the front door, sweating, out of breath. "The homelesses!" he yells, checking behind himself as if he's being chased. "They're going to get me!" Kaz sometimes overcalls danger, paranoia skewing his interpretations. A bump in the night is a monster, except it's the cat. A creak is a ghost, but this is an old stone house. A car that stops outside on the road is watching us until he sees it's delivering an Amazon package. It takes about an hour to figure out what he's saying. Reconstructing the story, it's possible that a group of punks on bikes tried to take his money and beat him up. Based on his distress, I figure at least some variant of the story is true. "They chased me," he said. "They said they were going to kill me."

*

I sit in the usual place across from the McFishTank. Kaz stands at the counter. Though his order is just one large cup, he must wait until all the customers before him are served their food in sequence. Black suckerfish, check. Smaller zebrafish flutter by, their genius of being outrageously, autistically pink. Spliced jellyfish DNA is a thing of wonder. A text from Janet pings: *Remember Aria dance tonight*, dance appearing as a woman in platform shoes and red dress doing something ambiguously ballroomy. Ahead of me, a woman who had been steadily talking into her phone for the past ten minutes says, "Why are you recording me?" I figure she's still talking into her phone, but soon realize she means me. She's now staring at me. She adds, "I said, stop recording me, you terrorist, you CANADIAN terrorist!" I respond, "Hey lady, I don't care about you, I'm checking my email." She says, "Oh yeah, well, I'm recording YOU now, you TERRORIST!" and then lifts her camera, ostentatiously pushing a button. I turn my gaze from the phone back to the glowing fish, eerie in the water, tank mutants meant for the top layer, the lone slumbering bottom-feeder beneath. Kaz arrives with Frink while smiling the anticipatory pleasure of soonbliss, his two tinctures precisely drawn out to the measure of two-thirds and a third. I turn back to the obviously psychotic lady who's recording me and use telepathy that she can probably hear. *Put down your phone, or I will feed it to you*. Message received. Angry-faced, twisting, she lurches up, revealing the soggy coat she was sitting on. A battered, overstuffed backpack holding a hundred things falls from the ledge behind, jostled by her movement. "Terrorist," she spits out, then leaves, performing several feints and dodges before picking her door.

*

In this busy McDonalds, all we need is Frink, but there's a press of people who wait at the counter for their orders. If not impatient, then the customers today are mad. The manager doesn't register their complaints anymore. Understaffed, it's dirty in the cooking area, as if they've stopped cleaning the floors and grills, all hands on food prep. Rather than try to sit near the aquarium, I stand next to Kaz, protecting him from the people, ensuring he can cut to the counter to get his cup when his number's called. Ahead of us, a mother and her teenaged daughter glare at the counter like everyone else, waiting for their food. They're forced apart by an overweight woman and a wiry man in a Chicago Bulls jersey, both bearing telltale signs of intellectual disability. On my quick read, it strikes me that the woman is the more cognitively able of the two, but the man is more physically able. Thin and quick, he pushes through the mother and daughter to get his food, crossing into their personal space in the process. He says, "I got it" loudly, with a lisp, making the mother and daughter grimace on their heels. When the couple leaves to find a table, I watch mother and daughter roll their eyes. Both make funny faces, and the daughter parodies a slight moan, as if she were nonverbal. I would be angry and admonish them for being mean, but instead I'm overcome. God, if my son could have what Bulls Jersey has. Kaz will experience the same mother-daughter routine a million more times from others in his life, but to get a drink with someone he loves, that he's in a real relationship with? I'd give anything for that. I'd trade my life for that.

LET US BE HONEST WITH ONE ANOTHER: TO THE CHILD WITH DISABILITY

Red crayon. Daddy credit card. Remote control.
Wavy flower. Sit mower. Snake.
Bean chair. Medicine. Poop.

Fairy tales are a standard means of instruction for children. But there might not be anyone in your life to tell you such stories, meaning that your fairy tale might involve someone tucking you into bed at night, or perhaps someone who loves you. Another strategy is required: let me tell you a fairy tale, the kind I've made up on the spot for my children. From the outset, I declare that this little tale is for all who can read it or hear it. I offer a fairy tale as personal dream, one in which you can save yourself. I write this tale after having suffered some as a child but surely not the most; I write to any suffering child, to acknowledge that you are there. In writing, I hope that you see (or hear) before you and in all other writing, that you are not alone.

Barnacles. Cloud. Gate.
Weebles. Child Care and Learning Centre. Big Park.
Scary vacuum. Poppy. Sidewalk chalk.

Years ago, my daughter Zee and I used to sit in bed and read long stories until she became old enough to read them to me. I pretended to fall asleep sitting up; she read to the end impeccably, orderly. (As I recall, Suess's *Bartholomew and the Oobleck* is a looooooong book.) As I sat on the bed, my eyes closed, did I ever think that things could be different?

C is for Cookie *song. Stroller. Friend.*
Soft blankie. Mommy. Lambo.
Thomas tank. Smile. Snowman.

We all need to be loved. When that need is frustrated or denied, we suffer. We grow in isolation, in strangeness; we become unusual unto ourselves, having sought sustenance at the roots and branches and having been denied. Who can teach us to love if we are born into neglect and abuse? This is one of the great problems of the world. So many of us are confused.

Peen M&Ms. TV. Juice.
Woodchip. Monarch. Moon.
Selfies. Window. Remote control.

Reading books to children at night, what could be more typical? This was the dream, a natural outcome of the actual dream I had as a child with disability. That we were unhappy at 429 Gardiner Street in Oromocto, New Brunswick, was no tragedy. What seems like a tragedy to me now is that we had no idea things could be different. My mother could have made other choices and gotten free; I could have been accommodated. And yet another tragedy is that I wonder, if we had done these things, would the alternate story have turned out happy? I wanted a family, and if I'm honest with you—as I am with myself every day, to stay alive—I wanted them to be normal.

1 Love. 2 Love. 3 Love.
Red crayon. Reggae potato. Red chippies.
CN Tower. Speed river. Presents.

This story cannot make your mother and father care for you. Perhaps you have no mother and father. This story cannot make an institution treat you well. It can't even make you care for yourself, but this story *is* intended to encourage that habit. I want you to be able to make fairy tales yourself, to understand that, even if in the abstract, the words that you read possess the power to care for you just as they did (and do) for me. Everything I've ever loved has been breathed into me first by the words that had to teach me how and why to love, never having been graced with an enduring, warm, emancipatory love as a child. Isn't that the dream, to be born into a loving home? I'm saying to you: love yourself into that home.

Earphones. Swimming pool. Pete the Cat!
Tank. Bumblebee. Wagon.
Splash pad. School. Prestonstylez.

Think, for a moment, of the classic scene: a mommy, a daddy, and a baby near a hearth in a log cabin. A castle. A plane. With a monkey. On a boat. A mommy. A daddy. A baby. In love (the condition is presupposed). Perhaps the mommy character says, *I love you, baby!* Yet she didn't need to, not really, because the love was already there, understood, love less in the words and pictures and more in the concept, the genre. And we, the disabled children, we feel the problem, the tug. This was often not our experience. Love was not understood. Instead, love was desperately sought, withheld, or compromised; for some of us, love was lacking.

Green cookies. Green tennis ball. Green Hulk.
Canada flag. Swing. Pew-pew Nerf gun.
Blue plastic pool. Feed Me Now! T-shirt. Goldfish.

Kaz and I didn't read stories the way I perfected with Zee, my eyes closing, me being the kid and Zee being the parent. He and I tried to read together, but he would kick, pull my hair, throw the book across the room. He couldn't sit still or understand why going to bed was important. Impervious to narrative delivered in this way, his attention span lasted, at most, tens of seconds until he was midway through elementary school. I read books to him long past the point where it made sense, Kaz in some corner of the room knocking over a block and a bright shiny board book in my hand, words coming out of my mouth, block soon to strike the wall near my head.

Rocketship. Orangutan. Heart.
Cat. Guitar. Dump truck.
Popsicle. Elmo. Dirt.

It was hard for me growing up, but it's also hard being alive now. It was and is difficult for many people. These words might not apply to some because their difference is respected and accommodated. Probably not perfectly, but enough that they grow into themselves because they are bathed in the loving environment they deserve. Every human being needs love from birth as both curse and gift. For those among us who can't protect or defend ourselves, the ones encouraged to accept ill-treatment as just and necessary, I write this tale for you. For us. We are not so alone because we are not so different. Different from them, yes, and distinct from one another. How could this matter?

Shape-O toy. Cake. Medication.
High five. Poop. Boogers.
Rain. Sandy beach. Sharpie.

Until Kaz turned twelve, I invented bedtime stories on the spot. Each story possessed three elements, and the game was to include the three elements humorously. At first, I had to suggest the pieces to him; in time, he'd remember some of them and offer items from his favourite stories from before. Near the end of our time together with bedtime stories, he'd devise his own list of three.

LED light strips on the bed. Cherry blossom tree. Pokémon Go.
Dollar drinks. Merch. Bone guy.
Poutine. Minecraft. Daddy's work.

Some might say I idealize a general case, that I take at face value storybooks for children depicting parents who cherish their offspring. I agree. That's exactly what I am doing, for a wind blows at the back of those books, a precondition that authors their eventual existence. I take the books seriously because taking them literally is the point. *You are loved,* the books say. *You are loved.* But reading them is quite strange when alone in one's room.

CN Tower sweater. Book too long to read. (Poop? Okay, poop.) Poop.
Garden peppers. Aria little sister. (No to Mom Hobgoblin.) (Yes, beautiful Zee.) Beautiful Zee.
Credit cards. M&M pillow. Uno.

It was hard for me. It was hard for you too. We understand the problem. We consider it to be a problem. We do not consider ourselves problems. It took us so long to unlearn the concept of self as problem.

Belly. Meteor. Clown.
Karate chop. Hose. Honey-glazed everything.
Batman. Balaclava. Bongo drums.

We have been shamed, mocked, and ridiculed. Some of us have even wanted to die because of that pain. Set apart from others, set apart by others, we hide from the world in the accurate anticipation of its cruel treatment. Our fairy tale, such as it is, begins to feel like the first half of *The Hunchback of Notre Dame*, without the passionate other life kept tantalizingly in view. We shelter in our room. Perhaps some screens.

Toast. Tumbleweed. Ninjas.
Shield. Fungus. Angel.
Phone. Police. Black hole.

Stories with Kaz always started the same way. For years, I said, *Once upon a time, there was a little boy, and his name was* ____. Kaz would fill in the blank with his name, and I would continue with the story. I was just creating a ritual, I thought; something amusing, predictable, able to bring sleep to Kaz in his way. Looking back, I realize I was teaching him about time, about how to structure experience. Others might naturally summarize events in a few sentences, compressing a complex narrative into a quick sketch. Kaz couldn't, but he did enjoy how the things he loved, silly things, could come together in a single story. I write all this as if I am imposing a retrospective plan upon things. I'm not. I'm just telling the story to myself as I tell the stories to Kaz. I have to make sense of this life. I have to take satisfaction and meaning where I can find it. My three-things stories itemize love, disability, and story itself. The tale I make of those items begins like this: *Once upon a time, there was a little boy, and his name was...*

Thursdays. Grandpa. Hospital.
Whistle. Bone guy. Idioglossia.
Church. Hail. Portables.

What good are fairy tales? That they contain monsters has always seemed hypocritical to me. There were times as a child when I was so tormented by others, by other children especially, that the prospect of monsters seemed like cheating. Nothing can prepare us for just how much pain is out there; if only monsters were real and life was simple! In life, we need to be loved, which means we need the humans that pass for monsters to provide what they cannot, to be other than they are. If only monstrousness were visible, a huge furry horrible talon-clacking beast sitting on the couch, remote in hand, or a sleeping vampire in fuzzy pajamas in the marital bed.

Toast. Tumbleweed. Ninjas.
Once upon a time, there was a little boy, and his name was ___.
"Kaz!"

Kaz wakes up one morning, maybe it'll be tomorrow morning, and he says to his daddy, *I want to eat some ninjas!* His daddy doesn't know what Kaz means. No one eats ninjas! Why can't the little boy known as Kaz eat some nice cereal with milk? Some toast with peanut butter? A muffin? His daddy asks, *Why do you want to eat ninjas? I don't think anyone has ninjas for breakfast. Not even for lunch, or for supper. First, ninjas aren't food. They're people. Kinda scary people. Why make them mad and try to eat them? And where will I find them? Maybe they would eat me before I could bring them to you!* Kaz says, *Humph. I'm hungry. ONLY NINJAS.* Kaz's dad says, *Couldn't I interest you in some nice toast? Toast that you eat every morning because you love toast every other morning except for this one?* Kaz shakes his head. *ONLY NINJAS,* he says again. Kaz's dad goes looking for some ninjas. *Ninjaaaaas!* he says. *Ninjaaaaas! Here ninjas, ninjas, ninjas.* Kaz gets hungrier the more his dad says the word "ninjas." He doesn't get hungrier one bit when his dad says the word "ninja." Only saying "ninjas" in its plural form makes him hungrier. And hungrier. And hungrier. And, he has to admit, Kaz also finds it a little bit funny too. Because ninjas is a funny word that's very fun to say. Kaz's dad goes into a corner of the room but doesn't find any ninjas. He looks in the closet, where he thinks ninjas are most likely to be, but no ninjas are there either. He looks out the window in case the ninjas are waiting to burst in silently, but no ninjas. Then he looks under the bed, where there are also no ninjas. But there are tumbleweeds! *Kaz, what are you doing to this room? My lord! There are so many tumbleweeds under your bed. You have a regular desert under there. What can we do about the horrible desertification of your room?*

Subway Surfers. Splash park. Ball on roof.
Sandy beach. Crocodilian. Ladder.
Zamboni. Spiderman. Wet noodle.

A secret: we *can* love ourselves, no matter how bad it has been. It is possible to escape the shameful prison created for us by ableism, but the only way that I know is through love.

One of the great distinctions I've learned about life is that certain actions are simple to understand but difficult to enact. If we have difficulty getting to the point where we can love ourselves, think of this: normativity tricked us into feeling as we do. Ableists tricked us to make us easier to control, into believing that we're not worth love. When I have wavered, and there have been many of those times, I think of how wrong it was for people to convince me that I was worthless and stupid. And then I once again feel like I belong on this earth. For those repeatedly convinced of their worthlessness, the feeling of belonging takes much practice.

Shield. Fungus. Angel.
Once upon a time, there was a little boy, and his name was ——.
"Kaz!"

The little boy named Kaz loved three things more in this world than anything else. I know what you're thinking. You're assuming he loved french fries. Or poutine. Or pizza. Maybe he loved his mom. Snow days! He loved toys and toys and toys. Well, you're wrong. These weren't his favourite things. Don't get me wrong. He liked toys. He liked it when school was cancelled. And yes, he liked fries, especially poutine. But did he LOVE them THE MOST? No. The thing he loved most was… fungus. Toe fungus, to be exact. He loved it when his fifth intertriginous space was slightly cracked and itchy because then he could chase his dad around and say *FUNGUS, FUNGUS, FUNGUS*, and his dad would scream. Kaz loves when his dad screams. One day Kaz was chasing around his daddy, giggle-screaming *FUNGUS, FUNGUS, FUNGUS*, when an angel came from on high, straight out of the sky and said, *Kaz! Why are you chasing your nice daddy so much? You are making him tired, and you are not going to sleep.* And Kaz said,

NO SLEEP. NO SLEEP. FUNGUS, FUNGUS, FUNGUS! He chased his dad around as the angel watched. *Well,* said Mr. Angel, *I am definitely on the grown-up's side here. Kaz, go to sleep.* Kaz said, *NO SLEEP! FUNGUS, FUNGUS, FUNGUS!* and chased his dad some more. Mr. Angel said, *Kaz, I know it is late, but I will have to turn up the brightness of the sun until you shield your eyes and can't chase your dad anymore.* And that's what Mr. Angel did! You might think he just told your dad to turn on the light switch, but that's not what happened at all. Mr. Angel flew into the light fixture and turned it on to super light power. It was so bright you had to shield your eyes, just like Mr. Angel said, and he kept the super light power on for so long that Kaz fell asleep.

Mailbox. Garbage can. (Poop! No, not poop this time. Not poop. Too much poop.) Train.
Spirit of Halloween! Andromeda galaxy. Canada.
Birthday cake. Buffets. Brown bears.

There are valuable things in the world that can help, that can slowly nurse us into believing that we belong, too. My bias is towards writing, and I recommend the reading/listening of/to books to everyone who can read or hear. By noticing beautiful things that become three-things stories, we can be shown a way to recover our sense of inherent value. The point is that if we begin to believe that the books placed in our path are the books from which we were meant to derive meaning, then we can resist all the punitive, derogatory messages.

Phone. Police. Black hole.
Once upon a time, there was a little boy, and his name was ____.
"Kaz!"

Kaz went to sleep five seconds ago. This Kaz wanted to grow up and be a policeman, so he dreamed of being a policeman. He wanted to catch bad guys and put them in jail. In his dream, he drove his police car back and forth across town, using handcuffs on all the criminals. But he got a phone call from the station that said there was a PG-13 in progress at the black hole. Kaz said, *What? A PG-13? What's that?* And the dispatcher said, *It's a notice that your dream right now might require parental guidance.* Then Dad, breaking the fourth wall, said, *Good thing I'm here!* Kaz didn't understand meta-Dad. He thought that his dad might be a criminal. *Hey Dad, you criminal! You criminal. Come here and go to jail.* So, Kaz's dad was going to jail when he asked from the back seat, Hey, Kaz. *Don't you have to go to the black hole?* Kaz said, *Where black hole?* And Dad said, *Just give me the keys and I'll take you there.* And the next thing Kaz knew, he woke up in the middle of the night, everything dark, daddy criminal nowhere to be seen.

Couch. Potato. Pumpkin.
Plastic straws. Mommy snuggle. Blanket fort.
Colour-by-number. Whole world all pink. Knife.

We need beautiful things as coordinates, as external manifestations of a loving force that act as reassurance, that we're going in the right direction. Sometimes the words are an expected part of the story. Sometimes there are other words. *I didn't eat potato*, Kaz says. *Ha, ha, ha. I eat ninjas. Ha, ha, ha and then…* Me: *Couch?* I suggest. *Couch!!! HA, HA, HA. Pumpkin came and said stop sitting on COUCH ha, ha, ha, cover eyes HA, HA, HA. I called police on Daddy ha, ha, ha, and BLACK HOLE HA, HA, HA, HA.*

Emergency Barney hand puppet. Mr. Muu Muu. Googly eyes.
SpongeBob stickers. (Yes, sure, the puffy kind.) Forward rolls.
Sleepovers.
Super Mario Kart. Water bottle. Being able to fly.

At the end of every story, Kaz tells me a follow-up story based on the three things. He often has trouble remembering what the three things are, and how he combines the three things often defies sense and grammar. Still, it seems to me that he brings the words together in a sentence or two as a way of re-experiencing the excitement of the earlier story. *Ha, ha, ha,* he'll say when he brings in one of the words, *Ha, ha, ha,* deriving pleasure from just invoking the object as a summoned thing or perhaps imagining a more complex narrative he can't communicate but which was in his mind.

Hole puncher. Herman the Worm. Walkie-talkie.
(Okay, bathroom. But no poop.) (Okay, peanut butter.)
Bicycle.
Mosquito. Yoghurt. Drums.

I carry these three-things stories in my mind wherever I go, accessing them to refresh my wonder of the world, viewing them as strange doors I might enter and exit, little portals into feelings and experiences I'd never had or never would have. I thought of the covers of books as doors. Now I know that books are the conditions of existence, the matter all around us, the point of being here. No one can prevent me from seeing what's beautiful. Recognizing the beautiful in literature and song is our best chance to remember that we're made of the same substance.

Pothole. Rock. (Can we do Lambo again? Yes.) Lambo.
Bubble machine. Leapfrog games. Shovel.
Trampoline. Snow. Peekaboo.

There are many ways to get us to believe in ourselves, to care for and love ourselves. The first step, though, is the beginning of a story. For the kids reading in their room, I hope you find the moral of a story meant for us: we *can* love ourselves, no matter how bad it has been in our lives. In the tale that you may write—one of us kills a dragon, another burns the warlock, yet another finds the magic egg—we don't heal, exactly. We change. We no longer conceive of ourselves as a problem. We solve the most difficult problem of all: we teach ourselves how to be autodidacts in love.

Love. Hate. Everything in between.
Circle. Square. Parallelogram.
Spoon. Bunk bed. Popcorn.

I write this tale to the children who could never hear these kinds of messages because they were seldom offered. To the children who were so encouraged to despise themselves that the occasional kindly messages from teachers and neighbours never registered. I write for desperate children who want to be loved but are instructed to hate themselves. To them, to us, I advise: there is a fairy tale. It has a monster we know and a love that we need. Imagine it and let the fairy tale end with us happy. Imagine it over and over until this happens. It might not happen, but it won't happen unless we can imagine. I believe that we can. Start with three things.

BUT NAMES WILL NEVER HURT ME

Retard. Retard. Retard. Retard. Retard. Retard. Retard.
Retard. Retard. Retard. Retard. Retard. Retard. Retard.
Retard. Retard. Retard. Retard. Retard. Retard. Retard.
Retard. Retard. Retard. Retard. Retard. Retard. Retard.
Retard. Retard. Retard. Retard. Retard. Retard. Retard.
Retard. Retard. Retard. Retard. Retard. Retard. Retard.
Retard. Retard. Retard. Retard. Retard. Retard. Retard.
Retard. Retard. Retard. Retard. Retard. Retard. Retard.
Retard. Retard. Retard. Retard. Retard. Retard. Retard.
Retard. Retard. Retard. Retard. Retard. Retard. Retard.
Retard. Retard. Retard. Retard. Retard. Retard. Retard.
Retard. Retard. Retard. Retard. Retard. Retard. Retard.
Retard. Retard. Retard. Retard. Retard. Retard. Retard.
Retard. Retard. Retard. Retard. Retard. Retard. Retard.
Retard. Retard. Retard. Retard. Retard. Retard. Retard.
Retard. Retard. Retard. Retard. Retard. Retard. Retard.
Retard. Retard. Retard. Retard. Retard. Retard. Retard.
Retard. Retard. Retard. Retard. Retard. Retard. Retard.
Retard. Retard. Retard. Retard. Retard. Retard. Retard.
Retard. Retard. Retard. Retard. Retard. Retard. Retard.
Retard. Retard. Retard. Retard. Retard. Retard. Retell.

NOTES AND ACKNOWLEDGEMENTS

Some essays in this book were published in the following places, with their editors in parentheses:

The Ampersand Review (Kennedy Cast)
Canadian Medical Association Journal (Monica Kidd, Barb Sibbald)
EVENT Magazine (Shashi Bhat)
Festival of Literary Diversity 5th Anniversary Program (Dominic Parisien)
The Fiddlehead (Rowan McCandless, Sue Sinclair)
Humber Literary Review (Leanne Milech)
The Malahat Review (Iain Higgins)
Maisonneuve (Daniel Viola)
Prairie Fire (Lindsey Childs)
Queen's Quarterly (Jamey Carson)
swamp pink (T Kira Māhealani Madden).
Who We Are: Identities in Contemporary Colonial Canada (Julie Sutherland)

"Chasing Goffman" was shortlisted both by the *New England Review* and the *Florida Review* in their 2024 nonfiction contests. "Chiron the Wounded Healer" was shortlisted for *Cutbank*'s 2025 Montana Prize in Nonfiction. "The Notebooks of Everything is Going to be Alright" was a finalist in *Passages North's* Ray Ventre Memorial Creative Nonfiction Prize. "McDonaldsing into the Future-Death" won the Gwen L. Martin Memorial Prize for Nonfiction. "Diagnosis Day" was included in Best Canadian Essays 2025. "The Two-Hit Hypothesis" won the Mimi Divinsky Award for History and Narrative in Family Medicine.

Intertext in "On Stigma" and "Goffman and Me" is from Erving Goffman's *Stigma: Notes on the Management of Spoiled Identity* (Englewood Cliffs, NJ: Prentice-Hall, 1963) and Lerita Coleman Brown's "Stigma: An Enigma Demystified" from *The Disability Studies Reader*, 4th Edition (2013). Photographs in "On Stigma" were sourced from my aunt, Barbara Ann Jamieson.

"Fatherhood-Trick" is quoted from *You May Not Take the Sad and Angry Consolations* (Goose Lane Editions, 2021).

Intertext in "Like Father /   / Like Son" is adapted from Blesson, A., & Cohen, J. S. (2020). Genetic Counseling in Neurodevelopmental Disorders. *Cold Spring Harbor Perspectives in Medicine*, 10 (4), a036533.

"Not the Smartest" is a developmental essay. Meaning: you may not like its message. Perhaps you will find yourself repelled by what you perceive as arrogance. If not that, then likely disgust at the depictions of internalized ableism and reenactment of trauma. Before you judge, though, ask yourself: isn't the first step of change to first see and honestly describe ugliness? Telling a perfect tale of "overcoming" with a tidy resolution, of Daddy Dearest superparenting, is false. To pretend that grace is perpetual when testifying about disabled life and parenting sanitizes reality. Moreover, such tales lead to more abuse and pain. You must consider mistakes and struggles to understand why some things are the way they are, the price of their being. You must understand how hard the work is, the toll it takes. You must reconcile the fact that you, too, are in development. For if you judge me, then you likely do so without ever having done the work that I have done and will continue to do until I die. I am not interested in the equivalent of parent sainthood, and I hope to honour all parents of disabled children by telling the truth. We speak of respite when we gather privately, just as we speak of love.

This book was written with financial assistance provided by the Ontario Arts Council.

Shane Neilson is a mad and autistic poet-physician who practices family medicine in Guelph, Ontario, and who teaches health humanities at the Waterloo Regional Campus of McMaster University. His prose has appeared in *The Walrus*, *Maisonneuve*, *Image*, the *Globe and Mail*, and many other places.

PRAISE FOR *WHAT TO FEEL, HOW TO FEEL*

"Poetic, unique, and captivating, Neilson's stunning disability treatise examines what it means to feel on the outside of societal acceptance, all while challenging perceptions of self. In this powerful read, Neilson expertly plays with structure to immerse the reader inside his brain, which is a beautiful, honest, and brilliant place to be."

— Dr. Kelly S. Thompson,
national bestselling memoirist of *Still, I Cannot Save You*

"*What to feel, how to feel* is at once honest and courageous confession, while also being a philosophical meditation. I cherish the way that Shane Neilson combines poetry and psychiatry, acknowledging that every poet is neurodivergent, and that we must be so to "harmonize" poetry's "long continuous chorale of wounds." Still, what is most *affective* about this de facto memoir is Neilson's obvious love, worry about, and care for his son. Read on and you will, most certainly, think differently about those who think differently."

— George Elliott Clarke,
Governor General's Award winning author of *Execution Poems*